BARRIE

BARRIE

HOW A RESCUE DOG
AND HER OWNER
SAVED EACH OTHER

SEÁN LAIDLAW

Hodder & Stoughton's policy is to use papers that are natural, renewable
and recyclable products and made from wood grown in sustainable
forests. The logging and manufacturing processes are expected to
conform to the environmental regulations of the country of origin.

Hodder & Stoughton Ltd
Carmelite House
50 Victoria Embankment
London EC4Y 0DZ

CORONET

First published in Great Britain in 2019 by Coronet
An Imprint of Hodder & Stoughton
An Hachette UK company

This paperback edition published in 2020

1

A CIP catalogue record for this title is available from the British Library

Paperback ISBN 9781529380682
Trade Paperback ISBN 9781529380668
eBook ISBN 9781529380675

Typeset in Minion Pro by Hewer Text UK Ltd, Edinburgh
Printed and bound in Great Britain by Clays Ltd, Elcograf S.p.A.

Hod   ewable
an   able
fo   d to
co   igin.

For Andy

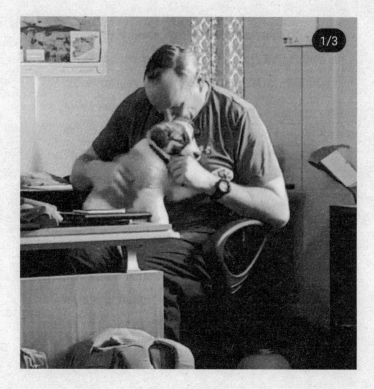

1

I first met Barry on an unremarkable Monday afternoon. It was overcast and a little bit chilly, which wasn't unusual in Syria around February. He was nestled stubbornly in a mountain of strewn rubble that had fallen from a nearby school. It looked like he was hiding, whimpering, under a slab of concrete the size of a door.

Barry was only small, and visibly frightened. I felt a deep sadness looking at this small dog, who was crying, surrounded by fragments of a school that was now scattered everywhere. He was a portrait of innocence, and I couldn't help but wonder what path in life had brought him to these crossroads.

I couldn't get a good look at him, but despite all the devastation that surrounded him, he seemed relatively unharmed. Relatively being the key word.

I've been a soldier for most of my adult life, and I have seen the terrible consequences that war can have for all it touches; our morning drives into Raqqa were a slideshow of such horrors. We'd pass miles of buildings scorched from years of bombing, homes whose walls were decorated with bullet holes. War is unrelenting, and Barry was born in the belly of the beast.

Barry's ears were a shade darker than the rest of his body, which was white all over but for his head, which was stained with splotches of black and brown. His ears sat comfortably on either side of his small round head. There was a layer of dust that covered him like a blanket; I could see it trembling on the surface of his fur.

'I'm scared too,' I said to him. He didn't know this, but when I was five, I was attacked by my neighbour's Rhodesian Ridgeback – mean old dog – and that experience had stuck with me, so I was a little apprehensive to say the least.

But I thought to myself, *to hell with it*. Worst case he bites me, and I tell everyone it was a massive dog that mauled me.

'Hi, I'm Sean. What's your name?' I asked, maybe a little hopefully.

He didn't respond, I mean, he's a dog, but he didn't even grant me the courtesy of a glance. His head remained fixed in position, firm and uncompromising. Instead, he gave me the cheekiest of side-eyes. *This is a sassy one*, I thought.

'You need a great name, a worthy name,' I said to him. I wanted him to have a cool name, none of these cutesy names like Rufflers or Marshmallow. Or Freckles – God, not Freckles. *That's not you*, I thought. I looked at him, inspecting him closely, and then it hit me.

'Barry. I'll call you Barry!' I said.

One of my team members – we were called Team 1 and comprised nine men – was actually called Barry, but as much as he wants to believe the dog was named after him, it isn't true.

Barry was now my mission. Despite all the sass he was showing me, it took just a cursory glance from him for us to reach the point of no return. I was smitten.

I'm thankful to have found him, not least because when I first heard him cry, I thought Barry was a Syrian child who was trapped, or possibly hurt.

We were at the end of a long day of work in Raqqa, previously ISIS's capital, where my team was tasked with creating a Green Zone, an area that had been cleared of IEDs and was safe for civilians.

We had blown up a tonne of shit throughout the day. ISIS were an unforgiving and deceitful bunch and they left plenty of traps and bombs for us to find. By 3 p.m. we had finished clearing the last of the IEDs in a government building off the banks of the Euphrates river in the south of the city. We were tired, and cold, as the sun was hiding behind whopping white clouds. We headed back across the river to a petrol station where our vehicles were parked, and enjoyed some warm chai tea.

When I say we blew up a tonne of shit, I mean *a lot*. I was a bomb disposal expert in the middle of the most bombed city in the world; the cacophony of explosions and gunfire was so consistent that it eventually just blended into the background. You just become used to it. Hearing an eardrum-shattering explosion in Syria won't raise most eyebrows but, that day, hearing Barry cry felt like being in an empty room where only his scream echoed all around you.

In bomb disposal there is a set process we go through from the point we find the IED up until we disarm or destroy it – typically the latter. There is always a moment of silence after an IED has been identified and the plan to disarm it set in motion. Essentially before the identified area becomes a Michael Bay movie set, we would stop and let everyone know what we're doing over the radio.

This is important, *very* important, because above all we need to ensure everyone's safety. Structure and organisation are critical if you want to survive out there. You don't want to be in a war zone and hear an unexpected explosion. Trust me, that is not what I would call a fun day out.

When things go awry, waiting on confirmation from other teams is a heart-pounding, gut-wrenching couple of minutes. You wait for the radio to start buzzing with casualty information, hoping for the eerie silence to be interrupted.

It's common sense, but it's still important we do this as we need to be 100 per cent certain that we're the only ones doing any blowing up of any kind.

Barry's crying broke that eerie silence. It was sudden and piercing. I immediately started sprinting towards the origin of the sound. As a soldier you have maybe a second to let yourself feel the emotions, but then you need to compose yourself and act. I believed this could become a rescue mission.

Raqqa is not as deserted as you might imagine – it's a somewhat bustling city. Or at least it felt that way. There was traffic on our way in each morning, there were markets, and children playing in the streets. More often than it should have ever been, we would find the bodies of children who took one wrong step and paid the ultimate price for it.

There's a small panic that sets off in your head, which is impossible to shut off, when you think a child could be in danger, but that's offset almost immediately by the realisation that they can still be saved. And that becomes the one and only thing you focus your mind on. This is your mission, this is what you've trained for.

I had a translator so that I could communicate with my Syrian boys, but in that moment he was wholly unnecessary. All nine of us began scanning the landscape, listening for another cry.

The sound had come from just a couple of hundred metres away from where our cars were parked, from this school that was completely caved in on all sides. Raqqa was not in good shape; the landscape was just rubble and dust for as far as the eye could see. Wind pushed through cracks and crevices and carried grey dirt around the city; it made an eerie sound, like a prolonged whisper.

I think Barry was trying to let us know where he was, as he let out another cry like a homing beacon.

'That way!' I bellowed, pointing towards a collection of rocks that cascaded down from the second floor of the school, forming a staircase for us to climb.

We had to patiently tread towards him, but we had not secured the area for IEDs yet, so the process of reaching him wasn't as quick as you might imagine. It wasn't like in the films, where you start sprinting frantically towards the casualty. It took a while. We continued to scan our surroundings for Barry, but also for any hints of a booby trap or wire on our path there.

It was a very common ISIS tactic to have a child scream to draw in first responders. This was a reality out here, one that still makes me sick to my stomach. Each step you take is more important than the last out in Syria, and we were always conscious of this fact.

After pushing through some more rubble, I finally found him shivering under a massive concrete plinth. I tucked my arms underneath it and was joined by three of my Syrian boys.

One more joined us to check under the plinth, to make sure there were no wires, tripwires, pressure switches or motion detectors there to surprise us. He lowered himself gently to the ground and caught a good glance. It was all clear.

'On three. One . . . two . . .'

On three we lifted the plinth and launched it over the top of the rubble. It was heavy, at least 100 kilos. Then, the few waves of sunshine left in the day swept over him, and revealed him to be not a Syrian child but a scared puppy.

It was a gruesome scene; he was surrounded by three other dogs and one big dog, which I assumed was his mother. Barry was the lone survivor of the unspeakable horror that unfolded around him. When I looked at him, he had this lonely expression on his face. I think, on reflection, I can say I felt that same quiet loneliness too. We often forget that war doesn't only devastate human lives, but all forms of life. Dogs are supposed to be man's best friend, but these dogs were never afforded that love and compassion. They only knew fear.

I had a biscuit with me, so I took it out and tried to negotiate. *He must be hungry*, I thought. Who'd reject a nice biscuit? But my attempts to tempt him with a bite were immediately shut down. Instead, he tried to bite me, three or four times. Ferocious little thing.

I wasn't ready to push too much – God knew he'd been through hell and back, and I didn't want to make him feel threatened in any way. Not that I was afraid of him; he was just a little puppy the size of a football, what would he do to me? But just in case, I wore my combat gloves, the extra-thick kind, and slowly transferred the biscuit towards him with medical clamps.

I wasn't scared of him, but when you're in a war zone it's generally a good mindset to be as cautious as possible. Okay, perhaps I *was* a little scared, just a little.

After some push-back, he reconsidered his position, shifting his round nose towards the biscuit and taking a tiny nibble. *Good call*, I thought. I ever-so-gently placed my hand – still protected by army-grade gloves – over his head and petted him softly. It was joy, pure unadulterated joy.

'Hello, Barry!' I said, rather enthusiastically. 'Who's a good boy?'

He had the most quizzical and confused look on his face as I repeated the question for the eleventh time. What can I say? I wasn't sure if he knew who the good boy in question was. On reflection, I was probably just some weird large shape yelling things at him, and he was just terrified of any loud noise.

He continued to ignore me even as he gobbled up my dinner snack, which I'd actually been really looking forward to eating. Once he started chomping away, the biscuit disappeared in just a few bites. Around me, I realised my entire team was in fits of laughter. I'm a rather big lad, with a big bushy beard, and big tattoos all over, so I don't think they quite expected my reaction. *They must not have known I was fluent in baby-talk*, I thought.

We all took turns to take a peek, and even in the short time we spent with Barry that day, he revealed a humanity in us all that wasn't always so clear in these parts of the world.

The good days in Syria were boring, the bad days were deadly. That day was different. There were smiles worthy of Colgate commercials plastered on all my boys' faces. 'Barry! Barry!' they sang. We forgot where we were for just a moment that afternoon. It's funny, sometimes I really miss those moments. Even though we were out there in the most unwelcoming of places, those feelings still resonate with me today.

As day turned to night, I realised I had to leave Raqqa and head back to camp. I had to leave him there, but I promised him I would be back.

'I'll see you very soon, Barry. Very, very soon.' I wanted that to be true so badly. I wasn't sure what Barry and I would share, or if we'd have a relationship at all, but he represented hope out there, and I wanted to keep that as close to me as possible.

I reached out to pat him once more, to make sure he felt some extra warmth and love. I didn't imagine he had experienced much affection in his young life, and I wasn't sure if I'd find him again. Yes, I lied to him, but a white lie can sometimes be good.

We left him with some water and set off to our camp. Tabqah was west of Raqqa, roughly one hour away, which gave me plenty of time to daydream about a future with Barry. I'm not trying to be a hopeless romantic, that's not who I am, but I was driving away into the sunset thinking about him.

At the base I couldn't stop telling everyone about Barry.

'He was just hidden under some rubble!' I'd exclaim, still genuinely incredulous about the fact that I'd found the dog. Andy and Digger, who would become godparents, of sorts, shared my excitement.

'What's his name?' Andy asked.

'Barry!' I replied. 'I'm going to try and find him again tomorrow.'

'You named the dog after Barry?' a somewhat puzzled Digger chimed in. 'Like *our teammate* Barry?'

It was a fun night with the lads. I spent the evening in the gym, as I usually did, but I couldn't stop thinking about the dog. *If he's there tomorrow, I'm bringing him back with me.*

I'd taken a couple of videos while I was out there, as I always documented everything I did in Syria. I posted a short video on Instagram of the discovery of Barry, and by the time people in the UK were awake, he was a bona fide superstar. Through the power of social media, a video of an abandoned puppy in Syria made its way to Essex, and the messages started pouring in.

My family, bless them, were completely floored by Barry. Non-stop questions and waves of love that made me feel a little jealous, I'm not going to lie. Suddenly there was a demand for Barry videos, and I was being told there was no way in hell I was leaving him out there by my friend Netty, who'd become Barry's mum.

That was the beginning of Barry Watch, and the beginning of a new life for the two of us.

2

I was completely lost before I joined the army.

I was a fresh-faced teenager from Essex coming to terms with all that life had to throw at him. The year was 2005. I had spiked-up 90s boy-band hair, never wore a shirt that fitted and – according to my teachers at school – had no discernible skills.

There are few feelings in the world as exhilarating as having your teachers doubt your capacity to succeed in life, it's just a wonderful feeling. A blissful sting that never quite goes away.

That's not entirely fair. My shortcomings in school were largely my own fault. I just couldn't hack it in a classroom. If you threw at me something practical, I'd give it a go. 'Sean is always great at the practical side of things, but never the academic.' Words my parents would come to hear from my teachers with regularity.

The classroom walls made me feel claustrophobic, and textbooks always disagreed with me. I wanted to do things, not just read about how they were done. I wanted to experience what the big world out there had in store for me.

You learn many valuable lessons in life; one lesson I learned as a seventeen-year-old was that placing school at the bottom of your priorities can severely limit your options going forward. Who could've seen that one coming?

See, while my mates were planning their lives beyond sixth form, I decided to drop out and find a job. Decided is perhaps too strong a word, as – at the time – my options were rather thin on the ground. An exciting future awaited those who were college- and uni-bound, but *what would I do with my student finance?* I wondered. Probably buy fluorescent shots of unidentified alcohol, and lots of them.

Richard Branson dropped out of school at fifteen, and he turned out all right. So I decided that a similar fate surely awaited me.

After I dropped out of school I got myself a job. While at work, I would find myself constantly thinking about that decision to leave school. It had made sense at the time. In life you need to love what you do and do what you love. And I hated school. And I believe hate is the opposite of love . . . so there was some logic to my decision-making – convoluted, but logic it was. I still remember one teacher back in sixth form once told me I'd never amount to anything. *I'll show her*, I thought to myself. *I'll bloody show her.*

That scene of redemption that played like a beautiful short film in my head was rudely interrupted by the sound of children running riot and screaming in what could only be described as a concerted effort to break the sound barrier. If they didn't succeed, they sure got close.

There I was, seventeen and enjoying a front-row seat for the immediate repercussions of my decision to leave school. For the measly fee of five pounds an hour, I had the privilege of entertaining children aged from one to twelve. A job where, more than anything, you realise that children have birthdays every single day.

I think we can agree that no kid in this country, or any country for that matter, dreams of one day working at a children's play space in Essex, performing party tricks with thick clown make-up lazily smeared over their unenthused face, for the minimum wage.

When you've got a deck of cards in one hand, and balloons that vaguely resemble animals in the other, you begin to strongly consider what life choices brought you here, and immediately do everything you can to not be there.

Love what you do, do what you love . . .

I had a fairly normal childhood growing up in Dagenham, in east London. My dad, Ian, was a data analyst. He was a hard worker and a pragmatist; a trait I think I inherited from him. I have his eyes, and his smile too. Or so I've been told. My mum, Karen, was a dinner lady at my school and tried her best to keep me out of trouble in my schooldays. My younger sister Rachel was as annoying and lovable as any sibling would be. We didn't like each other and then we did. My older sister Gemma would always look after me, and make sure she offered much of the wisdom she'd gained from being four years older than me. When she wasn't doing that, she was telling my parents to abandon me in an alleyway near a newspaper shop. She didn't take not being an only child well. We had a dog, Toby, a nosy little Yorkshire terrier.

We lived in a two-bedroom council house, on a street lined on either side with dishevelled homes, humdrum and toneless – ours had been broken into a couple of times when I was a kid. There were no parks, or anything resembling a park, so we used to pretend that the potholes on our street were the fresh-cut grass of Wembley and kick torn footballs about.

We moved to Romford when I was in secondary school.

I was a chronic underachiever. I was chubby, had braces that kept me from smiling too much, and was geeky but never smart.

In late 2007, after a number of failed jobs here and there, I decided to apply to join the British Army. Dad liked the idea – he'd been a cadet and had dreams to join the RAF as a pilot when he was a teenager – but Mum was less keen on her boy becoming a soldier. I remember walking into the living room after a long six-month search for a job to reveal the big news.

'I'm joining the army,' I said to them. *A good start*, I thought, straight to the point. Effective.

From my mother's side of the room a chorus of no's echoed across.

'No . . . No, no, no, no, no!'

Mum wasn't too excited about the idea, then. But you can't really blame her. This was at the peak of the Afghanistan

War, and suddenly the idea of blowing up balloons all day was a preferable career choice for her son when contrasted with blowing up bombs in the Middle East.

Dad, in typical Laidlaw fashion, simply looked at me and said, 'If you want to do it, go for it.'

And I did.

In the army I finally had an identity. I found something I was profoundly good at – I could tell people 'this is what I do' with pride, which was a totally new feeling for me.

I loved going through training, and it showed. I was focused. I got into amazing shape, I felt confident, I looked good. In my time at the Army Training Centre in Pirbright, Surrey, and the Gibraltar Barracks in Minley, I came away top of the class at all three phases of my training. I loved it. I loved the structure, I loved actually being *good* at something. No one could tell me I would amount to nothing in the army, and that feeling of uselessness vanished.

By 2009 I had successfully completed my training as a combat engineer, before qualifying to be a Communications Information Specialist with the 101 Royal Engineers. We specialised in bomb disposal, or explosive ordnance disposal (EOD) if we're to be technical about it.

My time with the Royal Engineers was varied; I spent two gruelling tours in Afghanistan but also had the privilege of travelling to countries like Belize, in Central America, Cyprus, Germany and Jordan. We were also involved with Operation Olympics, tasked with searching for bombs during the 2012 Summer Olympics in London. It felt good to be part of something, and most of all it felt good to be valued for what you did.

Our base was the Carver Barracks, in Saffron Walden, north Essex. Which was ideal for me, as it was just round the corner from my parents. To add to the sense of home, I found out that long before being converted into a training facility for the 101 Royal Engineers, Carver Barracks had been an air force base where, as a teenager, Dad had trained to be a pilot while he was in the cadets.

In 2011 I was sent on my first tour.

Afghanistan.

All the years of training will never prepare you for that conversation – don't get me wrong, I knew it was coming and I was mentally and physically prepared for it, but hearing it for the first time is a strange and foreign feeling.

I flew into Camp Bastion, Helmand Province, in southern Afghanistan, that summer for Herrick XIV – Operation Herrick was the codename for all British operations in Afghanistan.

On the journey to Afghanistan I spent most of the time visualising what it would be like there, in an actual war zone. I kept reminding myself of the last three years of training, every last detail that had been drilled into me from day one. *I was born to do this*, I repeated to myself. *No drama.*

When you first land and your boots touch the Afghan soil, they feel like they take on extra weight, like you're trudging through quicksand. You almost forget how to walk at first. There were seven of us on the team (we were called the C-IED Task Force). Tustain (first name Jack) and Deidre (whose name is actually Rory) were my best mates out there.

I was a sapper – essentially a private. Our job was to search for and clear mines in the battlefield, and to repair roads and bridges. The Taliban's second favourite pastime, after murdering and torturing, was to blow up bridges to make travelling an absolute nightmare. These guys were evil personified, but they were smart and organised. Most of all, they were ruthless.

Our base, Camp Bastion, was massive. It was more like a large town than a base – it was like they'd built a city like Reading in the middle of nowhere. Just a whole load of desert, and a totally functional town of 30,000 people from all over the world just placed right in the middle.

There were roads, irrigation ditches; we had hot water, internet. There was even a little economy going, as you had to pay for all the services in US dollars. Internet and phone calls were very expensive. So, if you received a phone call from me around 2011, just know you meant a lot to me.

Each task force had its own vehicle; in my second tour (Herrick XVIII and XIX) we had a Mitsubishi that we pimped out. See, it had no built-in radio, so we ordered one off Amazon – yes, they delivered out there, although it would take about a month for each order, no such thing as Amazon Prime out there unfortunately – and bungee-tied it to the central console so we could listen to BFBS (British Forces Broadcasting Service) on our trips. And the trips were long.That was when you really realised how massive this camp was. We had to be given a map and use GPS to get around, and it would take an age to get from site to site to get your gear.

On the American side of the base, I recall there being a Pizza Hut inside a shipping container. Us Brits didn't have such luxuries, although we did have a sort of coffee shop that was run by an old lady.

The first three or four weeks were rather uneventful; I think I expected to be dropped into a chaotic battlefield and to be immersed in this scary world that you'd seen in war films, but I'd say it was a far cry from all of that. I wound up spending most of my time getting to know the people at our camp: a lot of chatting, waiting around and cleaning my gun. Our guns were always clean.

Most days consisted of walking – a lot of walking – in heavy equipment. You either felt hot and wet, or cold and wet, at all times. Oh, and you were always sore. Hot, wet, cold and sore.

It was very loud on camp, with guns and explosions going off, helicopters and aircraft landing and departing every minute, so a lot of the time we'd end up screaming at each other. Which made speaking to your boys play out much like a conversation would in a nightclub back in Essex.

I didn't spend much time in Camp Bastion; instead I was stationed in thirty or forty different Forward Operating Bases. They were much smaller strategic bases that were scattered around the Helmand Province. A substantially stripped-down camp; less a town with plenty of amenities, and more a small fortification surrounded by four walls and barbed wire.

I was part of the HRF, which was like the Quick Reaction Force only with helicopters. We had a pager, and if we heard it ring we had ten minutes to get ourselves in the back of a helicopter and head into the vast unknown. Your brain was programmed to just be ready in an instant.

After taking two weeks of leave back home, I returned to Afghanistan. On my first day back I got called into the operations room, where I was told I was joining the Special Boat Service (SBS). The SBS are something else, they're a different level of badass. They're the people you see in films coming in on boats and helicopters to save the day.

This was when my tour took a stark turn; things got real. You're out there, and holy shit there's a whole war happening.

Don't get me wrong. As part of 40 Commando, we were told our primary objective was to support the SBS in 'hunting the fucking Taliban down'. Our patrols in the Helmand Province, the Taliban's stronghold, were terrifying. We knew that the Taliban were vicious, that each step you took could trigger an explosion that could kill you on the spot.

Out there, we had a target on our backs, and they threw everything they had to get us. Home-made bombs, hidden triggers, machine guns, snipers, women and children who'd been groomed to be suicide bombers. It was hell on earth. I'd lost two friends already. Each of us out there was fighting for something greater, but we were also fighting for each other. We knew we had to fight their cowardice with unwavering courage.

We completed countless tasks and missions in Afghanistan, but nothing like what we were about to do with the SBS. If the war out there was as linear as the First World War, then previously, with 40 Commando, I had been on the front line but now I was going to be miles ahead of it, in the distance, doing all sorts of under-the-radar stuff. Flying in for the first time, the only thing I remember hearing was the helicopter's rotor beating like a banging drum leading us into the corridors of war.

Truth be told, you don't really realise where you are and what you're doing when you're there, it's just a job. That's how we approached it. I don't think any of us really focused on the fact that we could get killed. We were aware of the risks, but you go out and you do what you've been trained to do.

I barely remember the first IED we found, burrowed under rocks, probably: a single step and that's one of us gone. I think we had a chat – Thorpey, Deidre and I – when we got back to camp and realised 'yeah, we actually did this.' It was exhilarating for a moment, and barely a memory the next.

It's all a bit absurd, because you're in this mad place, but you're walking around like it's a casual stroll in the park. Then, when you're in the middle of it all, you're just focused on your training, and what you need to do next to complete the objective. You have stretches of time where you are lulled into that sense of normality, where nothing is really happening, then times of extreme caution, and – on the tough days – it was complete chaos.

Bomb disposal is like a sick game of cat and mouse between us and the enemy. They set up traps with the most imaginative malevolence, and you need to outwit them. The explosive itself is only the tip of the iceberg, and even that is a damned puzzle to find. The detonator or trigger, that's where it gets tricky. Often, you're looking for a wire the size of a thread that has been hidden under rubble; other times the trigger is an infrared heat sensor – those are a different degree of evil. Weather is never your friend, and the terrain is a natural camouflage for anything they're trying to hide.

My squadron was always at the front. Some might say that's not a desirable place to be, but we had to be dauntless, and we wanted to be leading the way. It was pride, I think, as many of us had been told for most of our lives that we weren't good enough. That we weren't going to amount to anything. Here, we felt like we were saving the world. And we wanted to be at the front line to protect the people who trusted us.

I used a Horn detector, a long telescopic pole that would vibrate when it detected components of an IED, swinging it from side to side like a pendulum to find mines that were hidden under us. It was heavy, and possibly more important than any of my actual limbs. Beyond the detector, your instincts and training kick in. If you saw a pile of rocks stacked unnaturally, you'd be put on alert to the possibility that an IED was hidden near it. If anything felt off – sometimes it was just a feeling in your stomach – you paused. There's a time and place to take risks, and with IEDs that time is almost never.

Being part of the SBS was like being included in something secret, something only a few could experience. I was chosen to join them because of qualities I had shown in my training and in the field; I worked to get there. I earned it. At the end of the day no one was telling me I was worthless – the opposite; I had my boys and we were all appreciative of the fact that we had each other. For all the terrors that accompanied our time in Afghanistan, I could be proud of what I did, and who I did it with.

Becoming comfortable with the environment you're in, with your routine, is a fundamental part of your life as a soldier. It's a way to cope and survive out there. But there were days where it didn't feel like it was just a job, when it became painfully obvious that none of this was normal and that the stakes were higher than you'd maybe let yourself believe.

There are things you see, things you smell, things you feel when you're out there. As soldiers, we shut those feelings down, because if we didn't it would become plainly obvious that we existed in two separate worlds. The normal world everyone lives in, where people wake up for work, come home to their families and go to bed. Then our world, one where death always surrounded you. The ground we walked on was a graveyard, every last step we took out there. I don't think I fully realised this then; I couldn't allow myself to, none of us could, but there were nights when I trembled to sleep. There were nights when I wondered if I'd made the right choice joining the army, if this was all truly for a greater purpose or if it was just a mistake I'd made as a confused and lonely teenager.

We needed to live in a bubble to survive. We protected ourselves from the reality that existed around us, because otherwise we wouldn't make it out of there.

One morning we were en route to a village. Our intel was that a Taliban leader we wanted to arrest would be there. I was just a soldier, so we weren't privy to a lot of information that the SBS guys knew about – they were Special Forces who had secrets and clearance levels that protected details that were critical to their success.

While driving in, our vehicles came to a sudden halt. Our team leaders received a call from our bosses, and the immediate reaction of horror from my leaders told me all I needed to know. Something had gone terribly wrong.

Then, our leaders grouped us up and told us: there was a soldier, the details of whom were clouded and uncertain. He had left his camp and walked into this small Afghan town and, while there, he was captured by the Taliban. When you hear your fellow soldier has been captured by possibly the most wicked and vile terrorist organisation out there, you feel a sense of unparalleled urgency to save them.

The Taliban routinely massacred their own people. Senseless murder of Afghan men, women and children.

Grooming of children to become suicide bombers. *That was to their own people*, I thought. I couldn't even begin to imagine what fate would befall enemy soldiers.

In the brief that morning, we stood around in silence. We were instructed that everything was put on hold and that the focus was to find him, by whatever means necessary. We were given intel on his whereabouts, and as quickly as that we were in our gear and in our vehicles.

When you go on a job like this, there's a mix of emotions running through the team – there's a sense of duty to save your brother that is accompanied by this confidence and bravado that makes you feel like nothing can stop you. That nothing will stand between you and your goal. Then there's the dread, the goddamned dread. Like poison to the brain, you play through all the potential outcomes, each worse than the last. You shake that off, and you laugh it off. It's like practising a big speech in front of the mirror – you try to big yourself up. *You can do this, Sean, you can do this.*

Not long after we arrived in the town, we found him, or whatever shell of him was left. He was on his knees, on the bank of a river. He was stripped naked, he was listless. His eyes were empty. He had splinters in his fingers, he didn't have any of his nails. He had cuts all over him. It looked like they only stopped because they ran out of space to cut. He had several gunshot wounds to the head. I never found out his name, I blocked that shit out. It didn't happen. It was only years after that I even thought to look the guy up, I completely shut that episode out of my mind. I didn't question it, I didn't want to. I was ordered not to talk about it to my fellow soldiers once I was back in camp, so that firmed it up in my mind that I was to completely blank it.

We flew back. The mission was a success. You learn very quickly that in war success is a relative term.

A few weeks later, our main mission was complete and I was sent back to my original unit. I flew alone in the back of a US helicopter.

When I arrived back on camp, it was as if I'd never left. Everything resumed as usual, except I hadn't washed or shaved in a while.

The first thing I did was shower. Long-running showers were a godsend out there. It was just peaceful. The sound of the water pouring down blocked out everything else. It felt like you were cleaning yourself of everything that had happened. The showers were the one place out there where you could truly close your eyes, and imagine you were somewhere else. Hot steam would make you vanish in a white fog, and you felt like you could be anywhere, or nowhere.

I started working out. Bench presses. Leg presses. Deadlifts. You just go back to what you're there to do, your job. I was in Afghanistan to find and destroy IEDs. The next day we were all strapped into our gear, and ready for the next job. When you wake up in the morning, it's like a hard reset. It's like all the days that passed never happened.

I never spoke of that day until I got back to Camp Bastion a couple of weeks later, back with my usual team. The boys were talking about something they'd heard about. It was him.

'Yeah, I was there,' I said.

Those were my only and last words on it. No one asked anything further. It's an unspoken rule in the military, but we never dwell on these things too long. We'd rather just crack a joke, share some banter and move on. Survival was more than just a physical thing out there; it was mental, too.

When you're out there, you don't have time to rationalise what you're doing. You just know you've done your job. I was ensuring that my soldiers were safe, that civilians were safe, that our allies were safe from explosives that were placed by our enemy to kill us.

Back in camp the mood was always light, there was always banter between us. If your mate had his leg blown up that day, after he'd been seen to we would all be together taking the mick about his leg bandaged up in a tourniquet, because it helped us get through it all.

I made it out of my first tour in Afghanistan with my entire team. Everyone made it back. Some of the people we were there with didn't. One of the Americans, Peanut, an EOD technician, died while we were out there. An IED finally got the better of him. Also we lost Captain Lisa Head, a bomb disposal officer attached to another team in our squadron, and these are just to name a few.

Back in the UK, I stayed in the military, doing some bits here and there – training, mostly – and received my promotion to lance corporal. I enjoyed the added responsibility, and I especially felt comfortable training new recruits. I had a knack for motivating people and giving them confidence in their abilities. I was told when I was young that I would never amount to anything, and many of these young lads had been told the same thing.

Many of the boys who joined the army did so for the same reasons I did. We didn't quite know where we fitted into the jigsaw of life, and we struggled to feel like we had any worth to the world. I knew I could help them out of it, that I could drive them on, because I shared the same bumpy ride.

Training people isn't just about putting in the work or becoming immediately better. We all have it within us to achieve the unthinkable, and it's about tapping into that to motivate people to be their best selves. For much of my early life I believed I could never amount to anything, and that belief gets etched so deeply into your brain that, over time, that belief turns into fact.

I could help these kids because I was one of them. All they ever needed was for someone to believe in them.

In 2013 I put in my paperwork to leave the British Army. As much as the army had given me, I didn't want to spend my entire life in the military. I was great at what I did, and I revelled in the fact that I had finally found somewhere I fitted in, but deep down I knew I couldn't keep it up. I wanted to have a normal life, the life I saw my parents have growing up. I think part of me knew that the war would catch up with me someday, as it did with many of my friends.

I made plans, as a twenty-year-old, to settle down and start a family by the age of thirty. Away from the turbulence of military life. Maybe get a nice house with a garden. Have a barbecue on the weekends. Never hear a gunshot again. That would be nice, I supposed.

I was asked to do another tour, Herrick XVIII, which was sold to me as a four-and-a-half-month tour. It wound up lasting over eleven months. They needed me to train the next group of soldiers and bomb disposal teams, and I didn't need too much convincing to go back. I thought one last tour wouldn't be too bad; this was my area of expertise after all, and it would be a good farewell to a career that had been the only positive in my life thus far. There was also a lingering fear that pestered me at night. *What if all I am is a soldier?* It was a reality I didn't want to face just yet, so I delayed civilian life one last time.

Camp Bastion was even more impressive this time round. One day we were flying back from a task. It was dusk and we could just about see below us. Our Merlin helicopter was hovering above the camp when I felt someone nudging me: 'Fucking hell, look down.' A large, bald man, someone you wouldn't expect to be excited by such things, but he was right. *Fucking hell, what a sight to see.*

We poked our noses down, and Camp Bastion in all its glory was sprawled across miles of desert. I'm not sure if you can really spot the Great Wall from space, the internet often lies, but I think if you squinted hard enough you could probably see our camp.

They ramped up the amenities as well. A new area was built for private contractors, called Bastion Blue. There you could find a steakhouse, a sports bar (no alcohol), a pizzeria, even a KFC. They did everything they could to make you feel at home out there, as hard as that was. Whenever we had a long day, me, Kev, Tustain, Adam, Connor and the jocks would always go and have ourselves a massive rib-eye or T-bone steak. It was familiar, and it felt like a normal dinner out with mates.

It was the summer of 2014 now, and eleven months in Afghanistan had come and gone. I was ready to go home. Thankfully, despite being such a long tour – spanning across both Herrick XVII and XIX – it went by without a hitch. It was *okay*.

I took on a different role, focusing primarily on providing basic IED training to UN troops. I enjoyed that. I offered advice wherever possible and felt comfortable in that teaching role. For my efforts out there, where none of our troops were injured, I earned a Brigadier's Commendation after being sent home.

Flying back home, I wasn't sure what to expect. I was excited, I think, about what I could do with my life now. It had been a long time since I'd been home, even longer since I'd been a civilian.

The first bluebells began to bloom in the Saffron Walden woodlands, the first sign of spring's arrival. I hadn't seen flowers in almost a year and I'd forgotten how pleasant they were, and how nice they smelled.

It's a long flight, your last one, there's a stillness to it all. When I got back to the Carver Barracks, I walked in ready to say goodbye once and for all.

I spoke to my boss – Billy Sturgeon. He was a top bloke. He was my boss throughout my entire military career; tough as they come, but someone you wanted in your corner. Billy was the kind of guy who'd always want the best out of you, but never pussyfooted around any matters.

'You've just done a massive stint, lad. More than you had to,' he said to me, before pausing for a moment. 'Take your leave, take it all at once and do what you need to do – but do one thing for me, set yourself up for civilian life.'

I thought that was my last day as a soldier.

3

After eleven months in Afghanistan I can't tell you how nice it was to enjoy a pint of cheap lager with my dad. There's something cathartic about drinking tasteless beer in a classic English pub. *Oh how I've missed this*, I thought. We spoke a little about Afghanistan, but more about my plans for the rest of the year.

I was just excited to be around familiar surroundings again. I'd been away for so long, and really all I wanted to do was settle down. Dad agreed. I told him that I wanted to have a quieter existence.

'No drama,' I said to him. 'No drama.'

I had big ideas of a life far away from the turmoil of war – after all, I think most would agree the quality of life is considerably higher in east London than in Afghanistan. I was near my mum and dad, who for too long feared I wouldn't come back and were gleaming at the fact I was away from it all. I was seeing this beautiful girl, Nicola. She had blonde hair and large cat-like eyes and we had plans to start a family of our own.

'We'll get a nice house in Brentwood,' I used to tell her. 'Whatever we do, we'll settle down and have our own place.'

I wanted that for us.

I hoped for a rosy life as a civilian. I'd read about soldiers struggling to cope when they got back, and I knew many soldiers who'd suffered from PTSD, but I felt totally normal. I didn't think I would be affected by any of that. I had a clear vision for what I wanted to do, and those first few weeks felt remarkably upbeat.

So, when I found myself sleeping in my van, a single man, sometime in the summer of 2016, I couldn't help but wonder how I'd got there. The van itself wasn't too uncomfortable, all things considered. It was a black Vauxhall Vivaro and it was spacious and offered plenty of legroom. My company name was plastered on its side in white and red. BEYOND LIMITS, it read.

Beyond hope, I thought to myself. I'd been staring blankly at the glare coming from my phone screen for a good half-hour. I wasn't sure what I was doing. Not in that moment, not in any moment leading to that night.

It had been two years since I left the army, yet I felt more uneasy than ever before. I curled up into a ball, shut my eyes tightly and tried to get some sleep. Civilian life was a nightmare.

I don't know the exact circumstances that led me to that dark place, but it was a combination of things. I left the army as a skilled, dependable and ambitious man. I thought I would continue to be all those things, but as time went by I began to realise that I could only be those things as a soldier. As a civilian I was a teenager still, I was the same clueless kid smeared with clown paint and, frankly, I felt like a clown.

Some nights it felt like life had stopped, or paused, when I joined the army. And when I got back, everything I'd done up until that point was erased and my previous life resumed. My friends were in good jobs, getting married, starting a family. I was back at square one.

In my first few months back, I toyed with the idea of going to university. You get qualifications throughout your military career, so I had the option to do so. I went to a couple of open days to see what it was all about, and I considered a future as a paramedic. Ultimately, university still wasn't my cup of tea.

I was a qualified personal trainer. I got chatting one day with one of my best mates, Mitch Baldock – who is a firefighter – and we decided to create Beyond Limits. We didn't really know what we were doing, nor did we know how to run a business, but we thought to hell with it, let's start a fitness company. The one truly positive experience from Afghanistan that stuck with me was how comfortable I felt training people, and I thought this was something I might be good at in a setting where I wasn't getting shot at.

The first year was the toughest. I would start working at 6 a.m. and continue all the way till 10 p.m. I just really needed to keep myself occupied; I needed to work as much as I could because everything other than work was hellish. I would take client after client, and if we didn't have anyone to work out with, I just worked out on my own. I spent my life in the gym.

Both of us were struggling around this time. It was funny, because we founded our fitness company thinking our respective areas of expertise would be good things. I was a soldier and he was a firefighter. We thought those skills and mindsets would be uniquely positive. Yet, I still hadn't figured out what was going on in my head after Afghanistan, and Mitch was struggling mightily after the Grenfell Tower fire.

We were both brought up in the same way. It's funny to think now that we do know, but we were going through such similar things and never thought once to talk to each other about it. He was one of my best mates, my business partner, and neither of us could bring ourselves to openly talk about it. It just wasn't what we were supposed to do.

We were inexperienced, but we had big ambitions.

In the military there is a tangible progression: if you put in the work, put in the hours, you'll improve and work your way up. Life as a civilian offered you no such guarantees, and Mitch and I were new to all of this. I just figured if I kept working, something good was bound to happen.

At first, the company wasn't doing too well. We were losing money, I worked most of the time and I started to spiral. I couldn't understand why we weren't succeeding when we were putting the hours in. I couldn't focus, and I wanted to give up.

I felt lost, confused, like I used to feel when I was younger. After each hurdle, each fumble, I became more and more despondent and was unrecognisable as the person I'd become in the military.

As a soldier, if someone asked me what I did, I could proudly tell them I was in the army. I wasn't that person any more; it was like I lost my identity overnight. *Who was I?* I wondered. Maybe my teacher was right; maybe I really wouldn't amount to anything.

Then, like a light at the end of a long and dark tunnel, I got the best news of my life.

'Sean, I'm pregnant.'

There was a tremble in Nicola's voice as she said it. I think she was scared of what I would say. I don't think there are words in the English language that sang to me more than those. She was afraid that I would freak out when she told me, but I was beaming.

We kissed and held each other, and I never wanted to let go. There was fear, but the good kind, the kind of fear that makes you want to be better. The kind of fear I think I maybe needed in life; it was the same fear that made me as good as I was out there during the war.

I wanted to be a great dad, and I knew she'd be a great mum. Nothing else mattered.

Nic was pregnant with my child. We were going to start our family. All those issues I was having suddenly felt so small that I could just push them aside. I was going to become a father.

That house, the back garden, the barbecues on the week-end. It was all going to happen, everything was falling into place just as I'd imagined it in my head.

Everyone who knows me knows what I'm like around

kids, how badly I wanted a family. When Nic told me she was pregnant, it felt like the best day of my life; I called my mum and dad, I called anyone who'd pick up the phone.

Then, my castle collapsed almost as quickly as it had all been built. I spent years clearing IEDs, but life is a minefield without a manual.

It had only been a short few weeks since we learned of the good news, but we both knew something was wrong. Nic had been complaining about severe pain quite a bit, and that's when the alarm bells started ringing.

And then it happened. Nic had a miscarriage. I heard a long and flat ringing. I was in shock. All I knew was that we lost something that was ours that day. Something was stolen from us. I just wanted to hold Nic, let her know we would get through it together.

'We'll be all right,' I told her.

'I love you.'

'I love you, too.'

We cried, we cried until there were no more tears left.

The months that followed felt like I was repeatedly being hit by a freight train each morning. I felt pain, then I felt numb. Waking up felt unnatural, and I don't think either of us really knew how to cope or how to move on from it.

In the army we used to put these emotions inside a box. We had to complete our objectives first. We had a job to do.

That's what I did. I went to work. Nic and I still had bills to pay, she wasn't working and our financial troubles were not going away. I tried my best to support her emotionally, but I was in a dark place too; I just didn't realise yet how bad it was. Everything I should have been feeling, I shoved into the box.

We were drowning, but we weren't even trying to fight to survive. I just wanted to let go and sink to the bottom of the ocean. It felt like my arms were barely above the water and I couldn't breathe. I kept thinking, *I was going to be a father*. Nic and I were going to be a family. Every thought appeared to be in the past tense now; I didn't think there was a future for us any more.

I tried my best to be there for her, but I didn't know then just how fucked up my head was. I couldn't help her, because I could barely help myself. I felt like a hand grenade on the verge of exploding. And that box, that box was either going to open and eviscerate everything in its path, or I could hide it away, shut my eyes and keep on going.

Nic seemed very low and I tried to help, but nothing worked. It wasn't anyone's fault, really, but we were broken.

Then, slowly at first and then all at once, I stopped caring.

I was drinking six or seven days a week. Some days I would walk into the gym for a training session in my clothes from the night before, smelling like cheap whisky and unwashed clothes. I was doing other things I shouldn't have been doing, too. The days quickly became weeks that turned into months. I was wasting away. I was selfish. I couldn't control my mind, I couldn't control my environment. I couldn't control anything at this point. The only thing I could control was my body. So I found myself training two to three times a day. With us being in a body-building environment, everyone was taking some sort of performance-enhancing drug and it doesn't take a lot for someone to offer steroids. I usually turned these offers down. I'd never taken drugs or smoked in my life. It's not the type of person I was. But that person wasn't really working out so I did, eventually, say yes. At this point I may have looked like a good advert for working out, but it wouldn't have taken much to see I was a broken person just trying to take control of something.

I wasn't quite ready for the side-effects of steroids. I did research them but you only really find information about the physical side-effects like nipple soreness and acne. What wasn't highlighted was the mental side-effects. Not every case would be the same but I was pretty broken and depressed and it's like giving someone with anxiety a pill that makes them even more anxious. By this point I wasn't really me any more. I had a short fuse, I was on a whole new level of depression, and I was constantly looking in the mirror. Looking back, I looked like a *Love Island* contestant, with rippling abs, big chest and large shoulders, but all I could see was the chubby kid from school. Anger wasn't too far away. It didn't take too much to lose my temper, even with my loved ones and close family and friends, the people you wouldn't usually lose your temper with. As you can imagine, this put even more strain on a mentality that was already hanging by a thread. Now this doesn't excuse me from the bad decisions that I made but, looking back, it explains why I was making decisions that were out of character for me.

Nic deserved better than that. I think I did too. But nothing mattered after the miscarriage. *Why would it?* I thought. Suddenly everything slowed down. I had too much downtime where I was lost in my own thoughts.

Nic and I broke up, it was inevitable by then, and I felt so alone. We both did.

We still lived together for a bit and my parents stayed with us too, as they'd just sold their house and were waiting to move into their new place.

Nic really tried her best; she was never mean, even if she had every right to be. She still spoke to me and comforted me while we were sorting out this strange living arrangement. Through it all, she still loved me and made sure I was all right. But I felt like the world was crushing me. I didn't blame Nic for what happened, even if my actions didn't always reflect that; I was just so ready to be a father and when that was stripped away from me it felt like my entire world was vanishing before my own eyes.

Looking back, I didn't handle myself in a way I could ever be proud of. Nic deserved better than who I was in that moment. She needed me more than ever and I wasn't up to the task. I'll always regret that time in my life; I never said the right thing, I never did the right thing. I've learned, now, that I needed to be better in order to be there for the people I cared about. If I wasn't ready to open that box and access those emotions I'd so swiftly hidden away, I could never be emotionally available for anyone. And this scared me more than any war zone could ever.

Whenever I looked at her, it only reminded me of what we had lost. It was unfair to her, but it seemed like the concept of fairness was something of a fantasy in this world of ours.

I spent as much time as I could working, because if I was working, I didn't need to think about anything. But the nights were long and quiet, and I was frightened; all I could do was keep going.

One morning, after a workout session, James Stalley pulled me aside. He was a lad we trained with, a big guy, built like a bouncer.

'You look like shit,' he said. 'What's going on?'

I told him Nic and I had split up and that I'd opted to sleep in my van to escape our living arrangements and to stop her and my parents seeing the state I was in.

He looked at me, and just asked me to wait for an hour. I didn't even really know this guy, I just saw him in the gym in the morning. An hour later he comes back, he had a towel across his shoulders, and a set of keys gripped in his right hand.

'Here, take these.'

'What?' I had to double-take.

'I've just moved in with the missus,' he said. 'So, stay at mine for a couple of weeks while you sort yourself out.'

James would continue to check up on me even after I moved my few belongings into his old flat, and he wasn't alone in worrying.

Mitch came to speak to me that night.

'You're not okay, man,' he said.

'I'm fine, really. I just need to sort a few things out, but I'll be fine. No drama.'

Mitch knew a therapist who went to our gym, Kim, and he asked me to go and see her.

'She's great, man, really. Just give it a go.'

Dad had asked me to contact some veteran hotlines as well, but I didn't want to. I didn't think I needed to.

This was an eye-opener for me. It was so out of character for Mitch; he and I had gone through hell and back, and we never ever spoke of it. Not a peep. Not a passing mention. We always just went about our lives and kept trudging through. When Mitch, of all people, felt compelled to pull me aside and ask me to seek help, I knew I had to take the first steps towards figuring this thing out.

When he noticed something was wrong, it changed how I looked at it. *It must be bad*, I thought to myself. *Really, really, bad*. It wasn't how I was feeling that triggered it, it was the fact that he even mentioned it. It's difficult for men to talk about these things; there's a stigma attached to mental health that we seem wired to ignore at all costs. We went about our lives never speaking about our struggles, and for what?

I thought about how I felt when I first got back from Afghanistan, how I thought the idea that I might have any form of PTSD or mental health issues was silly, despite everything I'd read and known about other soldiers. As men, we'd rather refuse the truth that something is wrong in our heads than be emotionally vulnerable, even for a second. Because the moment we do, it's an admission of defeat.

When I needed a friend the most, Mitch came through for me. I realised that I couldn't avoid the reality that something in my head needed fixing.

'She's just going to chat with you, that's all. There won't be a big couch for you to lie down on, and strange art around her office.'

Mitch lied. There was a couch. But at least there was no strange art.

I saw Kim twice a week. She felt more like a mate than a therapist. I guess that's how all therapists are, so I don't know why the idea of seeing one had seemed so scary for so long. I think maybe it stemmed from a fear of confirmation that something was, in fact, terribly wrong with me. That was the most frightening part of it all, and Mitch helped nudge me in the right direction. He was used to saving lives – he was a firefighter after all.

I expected her to try to prise my brain open for examination, but she never did. We spoke for thirty minutes, and she took notes. She wasn't concerned with walking me through my problems, she just let me understand better how my brain works, and let me resolve them on my own.

For a little while therapy made everything worse, but I realised I needed to go through that. I'd never allowed myself to acknowledge any of the traumatic events in my life; instead I always just shoved them in the box and went back to work.

'The box is never going away, so you're either going to deal with the pain or you're not,' she would say, and she was right. Kim almost always said the right thing.

I was brought up to think that a man had to have a British stiff upper lip; shit happens, move on. Now we're coming away from that, to where we can talk about the shit that affects us. In the army we're taught to bottle it up, we're not allowed to be emotional. If we're ever upset, it's only behind closed doors. Speaking to other vets, I realised we're all going through the same processes.

The eleventh of November was the only day we were allowed to show emotions, for two minutes. On Armistice Day.

'That's bollocks. A hundred per cent, complete and utter bollocks,' Kim would interject. She taught me that it was okay to bawl your eyes out sometimes.

I cried thinking about Peanut. I cried thinking about Nic. I cried thinking about Afghanistan. Kim always let me cry, but she never consoled me. I always appreciated that about her. She allowed me to cry, and I felt like a man like I'd never felt before.

We spoke about Peanut once. About compartmentalisation. Big word, with even bigger ramifications. There was always a crackle in my voice when I spoke about him.

When he died we still had a mission to complete. One moment he was alive, speaking in that God-awful Yank accent we used to mock, and then he was dead. One wrong step. That's all it took to end a life for ever. He was one of the boys, but our mission wasn't finished. We had to continue, trudge on, forget it. We don't mourn him until we're allowed to mourn him.

I never used to let myself think about Peanut.

The most frightening conversations were about other soldiers. It's the elephant in the war room. I didn't feel suicidal, I don't think I ever have, but it was a lingering thought. *What if it happens to me? What if I become so fucked up and I don't realise it? Do the people who feel suicidal feel it all at once, or was it a progression?*

I saw Kim more and more throughout the year and she helped me access these emotions. When I opened the box, everything came out, every goddamned thing. It was scary. I was still in a bad place, but I took the first steps to becoming better. It was like ripping off the Band-Aid, only the wound hadn't even begun to heal, and blood was gushing everywhere. It was a pain that was necessary, because it was human.

Looking back at the decisions I made in those years, I can say I regretted 90 per cent of them. I regretted breaking up with Nic, I regretted all the stupid business decisions I made,

I regretted all the drunken evenings and hungover mornings. I regretted being so selfish.

Around this time, I told my parents I was going to turn my life around. I thought about those long nights in my van, those early mornings in the sweltering heat. Sneaking into the gym before anyone else so I could get showered. This was going to be a long and drawn-out process, but I wasn't going to try to do it all on my own.

Baby steps, I thought. The box had been opened, and in time I would be okay.

In October 2017 my friend Chris Harris, who was fondly known as H, died in Syria.

No drama.

4

'It's either initial success, or total failure.'

American EOD technicians used to say that. I kept thinking it over and over. *It's either initial success, or total failure.*
It's either initial success, or total failure. It's either initial
success, or total failure.

H was a badass, a search god; he could find anything,
anywhere. We'd done a tour together in Afghanistan and
before that he was in Iraq. He died in Syria, working with
a private contractor, clearing IEDs in Raqqa to make it
liveable for locals. He spent his last moments on this
earth risking his life to make it safe for others. A hero's
hero.

The bomb disposal community in the UK is tiny. There
are maybe a hundred of us, and we're a close-knit bunch.
We all know each other, or of each other. When H died, we
rallied together.

It was a cold morning in late October, winter hinting at its
arrival with a frosty gust that followed us around. Autumn
leaves coloured the ground a tinge of red, yellow and orange
that crackled when stepped on.

About forty or fifty of us were at the service that morning in Exeter, in south-west England. Matt Littlewood, or Matty, was there too. He had been working in Syria with H, with some other boys I knew. It was nice to see them again, it felt like meeting old school mates again.

There's a bond that only exists among soldiers. It's not because we're better than anyone else, not at all. It's just that only we know what we had to go through. Us bomb disposal guys, we lived the Hurt Locker. We lived that. That was all we knew. I spent almost a decade with mostly the same guys. At funerals, there was this feeling among us that we were survivors. When we paid our respects to our fallen friend, we also realised that we had tussled with death, and come away with our lives.

We were all happy to see each other. Outside in the car park we spent a good half-hour hugging each other, even laughing at times. There was some customary small talk ('How's the family?', 'How's the wife?', 'So what exactly are you up to these days?'), but we could all just talk frankly. Most of the guys were still in bomb disposal, but some were in the process of getting married and leaving the army.

I hated that I felt this way, but at the funeral I felt as normal as I'd felt in a long time. It felt good to see everyone, all my boys. Matty and I were in the same squadron in the British Army. We trained at Carver Barracks together, we went to Afghanistan together, and spent nearly a decade having neighbouring lockers. It was nice to go back to that world for a second; I didn't feel like I needed to hide, or change myself.

In a way I lived a sort of double life. Back at home, people saw me as this massive fuck-up. I was a fuck-up. I despised who I'd been these past three years, but most people thought that was normal. *That's just who Sean is.* But these guys, they never knew me before the army, and they didn't know me after. All they knew was Sean the soldier, and I much preferred being that guy.

I wasn't the only one who was struggling with civilian life, and it began to feel like all of us were itching to go back. Back to a place where at least there was structure, and some semblance of purpose. Yeah, there was the risk of death, but it seemed like the attractions far outweighed what life here had to offer us.

It was a dignified and understated funeral, worthy of a man like H. *He was one of us*, I couldn't stop thinking. *He was one of us.*

None of us cried at first, and then we all did.

I've been to many military funerals, and they never get easier. No father should ever have to bury their son, and as many times as we'll see it happen, it never feels normal.

H's dad spoke for a bit. He used to be a soldier too. He spoke of his son's bravery, of how proud he was of him.

One by one, we said our final goodbyes. *Goodnight, for the last time*, I said to him.

It was still strange to see so many tough men crying, but a funeral was one of the few times we were allowed to show those feelings. By the time of the wake, we had all composed ourselves and we spent the afternoon reminiscing about our time in training together, all the banter and shenanigans that accompanied that time. Most of us, if not all of us, had joined the army as angsty teenagers, so there were plenty of embarrassing stories to pass around.

Matty was a tall German-looking bloke. Most of the time he sported a thick blond beard. He had a large and slightly crooked nose. I was sitting by the bar when I felt his finger tap the back of my shoulder. He had something to ask me.

'We're missing one man,' he said, not-so-subtly hinting that I was that man.

We're a brotherhood, us bomb disposal guys, and I felt a responsibility to go, because it was a friend extending his hand. Maybe I needed to go too.

'This isn't the time to talk, but an offer is here if you want it.' He quickly introduced me to a man, I believe he was one of the directors at the contractors who were responsible for the clean-up of IEDs in Raqqa on behalf of the US State Department.

A couple of guys who'd overheard our conversation veered their heads over in my direction, both a little flushed, with pints in hand, and chimed in about Syria.

'It's not as bad as you think.'

'It's quite all right, actually.'

I didn't need much convincing. I was fighting my own battles here in the UK, losing mostly, and I needed an escape.

This was like the world throwing a lifejacket my way, and it couldn't have come at a more perfect time. I didn't have much money, Nic and I had split up, there was nothing keeping me in Essex. I knew I'd feel far more at home out there with my boys. A part of me wanted to stay for Mitch and Beyond Limits, but I rationalised it by thinking that with the money I made I could reinvest it into the company and create something more concrete. I trusted Mitch completely; I knew he didn't need me to be there for the day-to-day, and I'd always be in contact with them even in Syria.

It was like an opportunity to reset to the last place where I was okay, and maybe this was one way I could get myself right again. I could quash those feelings of worthlessness and go out there and do the one thing I knew how to do. I knew I could regain a sense of purpose out there.

I spoke to Matty again shortly after the funeral.

'I'm in. When do I start?'

By mid-January I was in Syria.

5

Airports are curious places. On a wintry morning in mid-January, London's bustling Heathrow Airport played host to hundreds of thousands of people shuffling around its grey epoxy-coated floors. The frost-covered glass panels were a reminder of the Christmas that had come and gone. There was always a hurried scene; it's funny how there's always this frenetic urgency to the way passengers act in an airport. I was relatively calm. *I'm only going to Syria of all places.*

Each person here, I thought, will be in a completely different place in the next few hours, sometimes new, sometimes familiar.

I, for my part, was going to be in Istanbul, in Turkey, in roughly three hours and fifty minutes. The first of five stops before arriving at my final destination: Tabqah, a city in eastern Syria.

Flying into a war zone (with a few stops in between, granted) on a commercial flight is bizarre, because you'll be sat beside a mum who is watching *Pitch Perfect 3* while trying to politely muffle her own laughter. And she's with her son, who himself is watching the new Star Wars movie.

They're probably going to Istanbul on holiday, like most people on this flight, while you're heading to a war zone. *I need a holiday*, I thought. *Maybe I should put the Star Wars film on . . .*

I took a second flight from Istanbul to Mardin, a city in south-eastern Turkey, where I was greeted by our fixer. He was the man, always a shady-looking bloke for some reason, who was going to get us across the border. This one was a man of a few words, but surely with many stories to tell. At this point I remember just wondering *where the fuck am I going?*

At the baggage reclaim I met what could only be another soldier, and more specifically another private contractor. It's just a look we all have. We're tall, broad, bearded. In the private contractor world, any white face is most likely going to be a fellow soldier.

His name was Chris, from Australia, where he was a bomb disposal expert in the army. There were also four Estonian dog handlers with us.

We threw our bags into the back of this snazzy white Land Cruiser, and the six of us strapped in for a day-long drive from Mardin to Erbil, the capital city of Iraqi Kurdistan.

On our way into Iraq our vehicle was escorted by two cars, one in front and one behind, loaded with fully automatic weapons *just in case*. Our vehicles were anything but inconspicuous.

Driving through Iraq was an unnervingly ordinary experience. I expected it to be completely ravaged and destroyed, but it was a normal place. It wasn't any different from driving around the M6 motorway, except there was a lot more sand and a few more potholes.

We stopped in Duhok and then Mosul, before finally arriving in our compound in Erbil, in a place called Atconz. The company was working for, along with other private contractors, had purchased houses and offices in this compound for its employees to stay in. It was nice, and very American-looking. The semi-detached homes were optimistically painted in different bright colours, much like what a kid's drawing of a row of houses would look like. We stayed here for a week, before eventually making our way to Syria.

The drive to Tabqah was a long one. This seemingly endless straight of paved road split the desert in half for 400 kilometres. The undulating road swooped up and down, following the rhythm of the Zagros Mountains that accompanied us to the north. At times, the road looked like it shot up into the sky. I don't think the driver turned the steering wheel for hours.

We crossed the Syrian border just north of Mosul, traversing the Tigris river. It was a mental operation, just absolutely bonkers. You had this wide-reaching river, whose rapid currents played a rugged tug-of-war with anything that dared to pass it. There was an outpost, with a man casually stationed beside it as if he was responsible for a log flume for children. People waited impatiently by the side of the banks, unfazed by the torrent of unwavering anger unleashed by the Tigris.

There was a bridge crossing the river that was held up with large water containers. White water containers. The bridge was about four hundred metres long, and these mad bastards would just drive over it as if it was nothing.

Multiple articulated lorries, which usually weigh over forty tonnes, and are about twenty metres in length, just casually drove over this bridge. Which, was floating on water containers.

The currents were violent, too, just to make things more interesting. Against all logic and reason, we got onto boats that were meant to transport us across to the other side.

Several families waited with us at the banks of the river, some of whom had brought the bare essentials with them while others had brought TVs and designer bags. It was an unusual scene. Although not too different from what I'd seen in Heathrow; there was that same distinct urgency.

When it was finally our turn to hop on, I thought to myself, *this might be the most unsafe thing I do here.* Unearthing bombs was one thing, but crossing this river was just absolutely mental. The boat had to turn against the current just to be able to go straight across. It was a bit like river-drifting. Or the worst water-park ride of all time.

'We're in Syria!' I exclaimed. It's not often you're relieved to be in a war zone, but after a week of travelling I just wanted to settle in. Plus, I'd survived the river crossing. That was, in my estimation, a very good thing.

There was one more stop, in a town called Manbij, where an old school had been converted into a training facility. We spent a couple of days there before finally driving into Tabqah.

I sent my dad videos of the training facility. He was always curious to see what I was getting up to, and where I was. Even when I was in Afghanistan, I always kept him in the loop.

Driving into Syria was nothing like Iraq. Whereas the latter had felt like a casual road trip in the desert, when we got to Syria it became immediately obvious that something terrible had devastated this place.

At first, we saw a few buildings that had collapsed, just an amuse-bouche to what we were about to see. As we drove deeper into Syrian territory, it was like a linear progression of horrors; the closer we got to Raqqa, the more devastation and destruction we witnessed. The towns were all the same shade of grey, sometimes offset by blackened patches – from explosions.

Some signs of life existed in the trees and shrubbery that occasionally poked out of the rubble. The trees were black and leafless. It looked like nothing could survive here, not even cockroaches.

At each Kurdish checkpoint the desolation got worse and worse. I couldn't help but imagine what these towns would have been like years ago, before Islamic State occupation, before the war. I wondered if parents brought their kids to school, and then went to work. If they'd come home after a long day and complain about their bosses being absolute knobs.

I'd never seen anything like this before in my life. In some areas the rubble and debris acted almost like a river, encroaching around whatever was left standing.

At our camp in Tabqah, a civilian base rather than a military one, I was introduced to some of the boys. Matty was there, and my new boss Mark Buswell, who was an ex-Royal Engineer and looked like a Daniel Craig and Gary Lineker lovechild, greeted me with a firm handshake.

I stayed in a shipping container that had been split down the middle and converted into two bedrooms. It was cosy. I set my things down and I felt comfortable again; I felt an eagerness to work again that I hadn't felt at all in my time back at home. I could start a routine, go back to what I knew. I lay on my bed that afternoon and took one big breath, and then another. There was a peacefulness to just lying there. *This is where I should be, this is where I belong.*

I felt a lightness that I hadn't felt in years.

My routine never changed while I was out there. Each morning it was the exact same.

0430. Wake up before sunrise.

0500. Brush my teeth, shower.

0530. Breakfast.

0700. Head to Raqqa.

In our morning briefs we'd discuss a step-by-step plan of what our job was for later that day. Typically, we would identify an area that we would then exhaustively search for IEDs. It could be an area, a building or a road. If it was successfully cleared it would be marked as a Green Zone, which meant it was completely safe for civilians.

Our drives into Raqqa took a couple of hours. One, because ISIS blew up all the bridges leading into the city during their occupation. Two, because despite what you would expect, there were a surprisingly high number of civilians driving in and out of the city.

We drove a different route each morning, a precautionary measure. The places we'd pass offered a small look into what Syria may have been before all of this. There were always children playing on the side of the street. When they would see us, they would always greet us with two fingers raised firmly in the air. A peace sign, I was told. One raised index finger, however, meant they were ISIS militants. A child, barely four foot tall, giving an ISIS militant sign. This was a place where innocence was stripped from those who never asked to be in this fight, yet were often the ones to pay the ultimate price.

Both in and around Raqqa were several busy markets. One of my favourites, located on a road that might have been a high street of sorts in its heyday, featured this small colourful restaurant stall. Its tables and chairs, coloured in warm and vivacious red, blue and yellow, were a welcome change from its dull surroundings. The geezer used to sell the best falafel I'd ever eaten. Never seen a man so happy in my life, and as well he should be – he made deep-fried gold. Eating falafel today still brings me back to that stall, although nothing will ever compare.

Raqqa and its people were ready to return to their normal lives, and I was here to help. This was different from Afghanistan, as we were here on a humanitarian mission to make Raqqa safe for its citizens.

The city had been consumed by a battle that lasted four months, ending in October the previous year when the Syrian Democratic Forces (SDF) defeated ISIS, with the help of British, American, German and French forces.

ISIS may have been defeated, but the traces of their evil could still be found hidden away under every rock, every crevice and every building.

On my first day in Raqqa we found more IEDs than in my previous eight years in the military. The city was infested with them. In one single building we found around fifteen IEDs. It took an entire week to clear the area.

I settled in almost instantly. When I got my military gear on, it felt like a second skin. After the debrief, I spent the night in the gym with Andy, Tricky and Matty. They were to become my gym partners. I was still running my fitness company, so I would film my workouts, but the lot of them would always ruin my takes. It's hard to explain, but there was something so gratifying about being mocked without it piercing through your soul. Back home, I was such a mess that any jokes about the state of my life, or what I was doing, just broke me to my core. Now, here, I could laugh along with it.

The following morning it was the same again. I was up like a spring at 4:30 a.m., when the sun had yet to rise. I brushed my teeth, I showered. We had a shower block with running hot water.

There was a brilliant kitchen, like something out of a five-star hotel. On this particular morning, I opted for porridge, but other times I treated myself to a proper fry-up. Bacon, sausage, eggs, toast and the lot. Anything we wanted to eat, they could make. Although there was something not right with their bacon, it just wasn't bacon. It tasted all right, but I could sniff out an impostor bacon from a mile away.

Like clockwork we would all meet at our vehicles for our morning briefing, just me and my team, and by 6 a.m. we were ready to drive into Raqqa.

Our cars, all white Land Cruisers, were always ready and lined up in the exact order they had to be in. Before we got in, I always checked my team's front and back armour plates. I'd punch them lightly to see if they were fitted and ready.

Everyone was checked for first aid kits; everyone had to have their own. We had a motto: My first aid kit is for you, yours is for me. Out there we had to protect each other.

We didn't mess around with our morning routine. We had a rigid structure, and everything was planned and considered beforehand. We knew exactly where we were going, we took pictures and videos with a drone of anything we did, and at the end of the day I wrote a detailed report of what happened.

First in the car was my translator, Fareed. He was an intelligent bloke, I think he had a few degrees, and he always spoke with a soft and collected tone. None of the Syrians I trained spoke English, so he was fundamental to our operation. He was a good guy, and while no one deserved to live in a war zone, Fareed was one of those guys who particularly made me think long and hard about how damning the place you're born can be. He was smarter than I was, and hard-working, and everything any good person would want to be. Yet his home had been destroyed, and this was his reality.

When we arrived at the area we were clearing, the atmosphere was generally quite relaxed. In bomb disposal, we refer to the period when we approach an IED as 'the long walk'. I learned pretty quickly, by day two in Syria, that I would be having many long walks here. If you ever see a bomb disposal guy put 'I love long walks' on his Tinder profile, you know he means it.

That afternoon we were tasked with searching a compound that was part of a grain silo facility. There were two entrances to it. One of our searchers walked in from the right-hand side and saw a box where a box really shouldn't have been. He was right – inside the box was an explosive and some acid. The explosive was triggered by a PIR, which is a small black infrared sensor.

We spotted it at the bottom of the box facing the door. This is a fun old device. It works on a three-strike system, and tracks heat rather than movement. Our searcher stood still in front of it. That was strike one.

I looked him straight in the eye. Sweat was gushing down his forehead.

'Fareed, tell him to run towards me. There's nothing he can do now.' I waved my hands to indicate he should come over.

There was a moment that felt like an eternity. He looked at me. I looked at him. Sweat continued to trickle down his cheeks and onto his neck.

In a moment of courage, adrenaline and a little madness, he shot out of the building and threw himself to the ground. He was on his back, I knew his heart was beating as fast and strong as a thousand galloping horses. The dust settled around him, no explosion was triggered, and he burst out into laughter.

He had a look on his face that screamed 'oh shit, that was a close one', and we all smiled at him. *You're a lucky bugger*, I thought. Our job didn't end there however. We had to identify the IED and see if we could do anything to disarm or destroy it.

I have mentioned more than once that ISIS were evil, and this device was no different. The box hid the explosive and the sensor was the trigger. The goal was to kill the first group of people who walked in with the explosion, while the acid would splash across, hitting everything in its radius. Flesh-destroying, bone-melting, burning acid. If you felt lucky you'd survived the explosion, what came next was a hundred times worse.

It was really savage. I don't know who pissed them off.

I decided to check the other side of the house, through the left entrance, to see if there were any other IEDs lying about. I didn't want to come in through the other door, as this building was clearly a death trap; if they had a sensor at one entrance, they probably had one at the other. I tried to be sneaky and attempted to gain access to the room through a window, and pushed myself into it, and my body was hanging out the other side of it when I saw it. Another goddamned explosive. Cautiously, I entered the building, feeling like MacGyver in the process.

I scanned the ground, the walls, just about every surface area, for the trigger. I had to figure out what would set it off, or this day was going to have an un-ideal end to it. There was still the PIR in the other room to worry about, and my instinct was to look for another small black sensor in this room. Unfortunately, with IEDs, there aren't any set manuals that tell you what to do; these fuckers were creative.

I looked around, carefully moving an inch or two at a time. Then, I radioed Matty.

'Hey, mate, get everyone out of here.'

'How bad is it?'

'It's bad.'

'Worse than the last one?'

'Worse.'

I'd spotted the tripwire. It was thin and barely visible. We called them crush wires, because they looked like the wires that connect under your keyboard. They are almost impossible to see; I used to throw the wires back into the ground during training sessions to see if the boys could spot them. Most of the time they would accuse me of not having thrown them. These things were scattered just about everywhere in Syria.

There was also another PIR, just in case the tripwire didn't do the trick. Their goal was to kill and injure as many of us as possible, knowing that, after the first explosion and the acid shower that followed, there would be a frantic panic to get to safety. If you survived that, you would probably run into the other room for cover, and you would be royally fucked. If the explosion didn't kill us, the building would probably just collapse around us and crush us or trap us, while all the time the acid continued to eat into our skin.

Just like that, it could have been over.

Bomb disposal is a mixed bag; sometimes it's just snipping a red wire, other times you can even hold the explosive in your hand as it is completely harmless without a trigger. On more extraordinary occasions, like that afternoon, you see your life dangle on a single wire.

This is what I signed up for.

Later that evening we went through all the details of the day with my boss Mark, and the Syrian leader. We went through everything with a fine-tooth comb each night. Every last detail.

I took a long shower that evening. *Not bad for the first week*, I thought. You couldn't help but laugh. The fucked-up thing was that I felt serene. I was less scared out there than I was back in Essex.

I was hopeful. I thought that working with a team of people who were like me would help me sort out some of the issues I'd been struggling with. I could be better here in Syria. I was training people, I had a purpose, and people looked to me for help. I was a point of reference for so many of the civilians who wanted to live in their homes without fear.

A month later I met Barry for the first time. The four days that followed would change the course of both of our lives for ever.

6

The morning after I met Barry, I awoke knowing that I had an appointment with my furry friend later that day. I knew there was a chance I wouldn't find him again, and that made me uneasy. I hoped he would be there, and that he wouldn't be scared. I felt almost too overwrought to have breakfast, but quickly ate my porridge and packed some biscuits for Barry.

In the month that I had been in Syria, until that point my morning routine had never wavered. Not once. It was the same each day; down to the minute I woke up and the number of eggs I took with my fry-up (two). Now, my morning routine had a new addition. Some extra sausages and biscuits – I was packing lunch for two.

I was more upbeat than usual on our drive into Raqqa. We didn't have a radio, so I used to record the previous day's BBC Radio 1 Breakfast Show with Greg James to listen to on our journeys in. It was nice, it made me feel like I had a little bit from back home with me.

We were still searching the same area we'd passed through the day before, but we shifted our focus on an apartment on the main street adjacent to the school where we'd found Barry. *We'll have a chance to pass by*, I thought. *Definitely.* The areas we searched typically took about a week or two to clear before we could mark them as a Green Zone, so I knew we had some time to interact with Barry.

One of our Syrians always stayed back, near where we parked our vehicles, just north of the school. He was the guy who would have to run towards us with a medic if anything went wrong. He also made us delicious chai tea every day, so we came to call him tea man. Today, he had an additional responsibility.

'Your job is to radio me if you see Barry, okay?' I looked to Fareed, urging him to translate it to tea man.

'Okay!' he said, using the little English he did know, with a smile and two thumbs pointed up. *Excellent.*

When we were done for the day, I shifted my attention to finding Barry. I retraced my steps back to the site of the school, carefully treading over the same path I had previously. We hadn't cleared the area, still, so I had to tiptoe around. I looked, and I looked, but he wasn't there any more. Maybe when we threw the pillar over, we threw away his cover too. Maybe we'd scared him away.

He could be anywhere by now. Unfortunately, tea man never radioed in at any point during the day. I'd been cautiously optimistic to hear his voice, but he said he didn't see him anywhere. It was disappointing, and completely flattened my mood. He was there with his patented chai tea: 'Wonderful, as usual, brother,' I said to him. I offered him a half-smile; Barry was still stuck at the back of my mind. Maybe it was too much of a Hollywoodian script for me to find him; that's not how things work in real life.

There wasn't much of an emotional attachment at first. *It's fine, yes, it's not a big deal. I barely knew him. He was probably full of diseases and rabies and horrid things like that.* I had to try to reason with myself.

We were doing important work out there, and I had a responsibility to my Syrian boys to train them up to identify and destroy IEDs. All eight of them counted on me. Clearing the IEDs was the top priority for us, and as much as I wanted to put all my efforts into finding this dog, it couldn't compromise our primary obje—

'Barry! Barry! Barry!' one of my Syrian boys shouted, breaking my reverie. I snapped out of it and looked at him. He was flailing his arms towards the outer wall of the school compound. I lit up like a Christmas tree. All that nonsense I was spouting about emotional attachment, rabies and compromise flew right out the window. He was smart – he'd hidden in a more secluded area, where the wind at night wouldn't hit with as much ferocity.

He'd moved into a small makeshift grotto made of debris, a segment of a fence and some fallen branches that acted as a roof. He appeared to be stuck in a Barry-shaped hole he'd squeezed himself through.

I popped round to say hello. He must have been wondering who this geezer was who wouldn't leave him alone. I was a proper stalker.

In the commotion I dropped one of the biscuits on the ground, but it was all right, I came prepared. I had multiple biscuits – that's that army training coming to good use.

I placed the biscuit near his head and watched him ignore it for twenty minutes. He refused to move. His face rested idly on a rusty rail that crossed over his lodging. He was still shivering. I placed a blanket on top of him. It would keep him warm and maybe hide him from any potential danger.

'You've got nothing to worry about,' I said to him, all the while trying to entice him with the biscuit. 'You've got to eat up, Barry, it's good for you.'

I felt like my nan trying to get me to eat my vegetables. I even tried to do the aeroplane thing to get him to have a nibble, but he continued to ignore me. I wasn't much different as a kid, so I could understand what he was feeling.

He wasn't ready to trust me yet, but why would he when the world had offered him little reason to trust anyone? I had to take a leap of faith, if he was ever to take one on me. So, despite my better judgement, I extended my hand – gloveless and bare – and softly petted his head, then glided my hand across his back. I liked petting him. It felt . . . *Right*.

'We're going to be good friends,' I whispered, continuing to pet his head. I wanted to stay and pet him all day.

I realised that he needed his space, he was still trying to understand this mad world that surrounded him. I left the biscuit next to him, and some water. Even if he didn't trust anyone, surely his need for hydration would supersede any scepticism.

On our drive back I knew this wasn't just some day like any other, as he wasn't a dog like any other. I still debriefed my team, I still wrote my report, I still worked out and showered. It was all the same as it always was, but I felt different. I felt hopeful.

The following day, day three of Barry Watch for the faithful few who followed the events closely on Instagram, he managed to scurry up to the top of the grotto, to its very peak, and basked in the rare sun that glowed that morning. He wasn't hiding, he was sunbathing. *Cheeky little dog*, I thought.

It was February in Syria, and it was common for the temperature to dip below zero degrees during the night, but on some afternoons the cold was replaced with a warm cloak of sunshine, and young Barry was on the scene to take advantage of the warmth.

He's already British, I thought. He really looked like he was on the beach, getting his tan on. It reminded me of home, where if there was even a hint of sunshine in a season that wasn't summer, anything above 18 degrees, people would flock out of their homes in their favourite summer outfits.

Barry kept his eyes firmly shut, as if to say *Do not disturb*. I don't know if he'd felt much peacefulness or tranquillity in his young life, but he seemed blissfully happy in that moment.

We were still busy at work – the Green Zone wasn't going to clear itself – but whenever I could, I would dart back over to where he was to give him a biscuit, or a sausage, or just to say hello. My entire team was feeling the Barry-fever too; he had a warm quality about him that put a smile on everyone's face.

I'd set up a date with Barry after work. *No one can resist an after-work drink, not even Barry.* I brought him a cup of water (I know, I know), but he was fast asleep. His breathing was relaxed. I could see his small lungs fill up with air as his teeny-tiny body puffed up after each long breath. He was calmer, and he'd stopped shivering, maybe because it was warmer, but maybe because he felt safer.

I petted him some more before leaving and he woke to my rough and calloused hand caressing him. He took his time to open his eyes, gazing at me not with contempt but with curiosity. He was drowsy from the little siesta he'd just had, but he seemed to like it when I petted him.

I think Barry knew now that I was his friend. He lowered his walls for the first time and looked me straight in the eye. We'd made some eye contact before, but this was the first time he really looked at me.

I hadn't got such a good look at him before, nor he at me. He had black pearly eyes that were round like you'd find on a teddy bear. The rest of him was quite teddy-bear-like as well. He was fluffy and cuddly, and his almost perfect roundness was an invitation to hold him tightly in your arms. He made you feel an innate happiness that reminded me of being a boy again, innocent and loving.

We worked five days a week, between Saturday and Thursday, so I woke up on Thursday morning, or day four of Barry Watch, with the intention of bringing Barry back to base with me.

The night before, I'd prepared the vessel in which we would transport him. It was a blue plastic fruit basket fitted inside a cardboard box, which was very kindly donated to me by my catering manager. Five-star service for my Barry. And yes, he was already *my* Barry by this point.

At the end of our morning brief I brought my team together and told them I needed to add one last thing.

'We all know about Barry. Today, we're going to evacuate him and bring him back to our base.'

This was a bit off-book, but if we were going to do this, we had to plan for it. We were still in a war zone, and as much as Barry made us forget it, there were dangers we needed to be equipped to react to. Every single thing we did out there was structured and planned, and Barry was no different.

Everyone was made aware of which vehicle they would be in, and where we would place Barry after he was secured.

'No matter what,' I said, 'we bring Barry home.'

I normally took videos of Barry when I saw him in Raqqa, but today was a special day, the finale of Barry Watch, so I documented our trip in.

On the route we took that morning we passed by a mass grave. A ditch with hundreds of dead bodies. There were quite a few mass graves in Raqqa, but as often as I saw them, they never failed to creep me out. There was a car parked on the side of the road, and when I slowed down to have a gander, I saw there was a man in a vest sat inside. He had a bullet hole going straight through his forehead. *A little ominous,* I thought.

After a routine day, still clearing IEDs in the same area, we were ready to get Barry. He was still in his same spot, hiding from the world, but not from me. When I approached him he looked at me – maybe he knew I was taking him home with me today. I offered him some food again – a sausage – which he ate without hesitation. Perhaps a sign that he trusted me. Everyone loves a good sausage; I remember when I was a kid I'd inhale portions of bangers and mash like a vacuum cleaner.

On 1 March 2018, at around midday, I held Barry in my arms for the very first time. I wasn't sure how to pick him up, but I figured the best method was to put my hands under his two front legs and lift him up like Simba. He had a confused look on his face: *What is this man doing?*

It's strange to say, but I don't think I'd ever held a dog in my arms before Barry, but he fitted perfectly. I cradled him in my arms and, looking down at his cute face, that's when I knew he was my little boy and I was his dad. He felt warm in my arms, like a soft pillowy dough.

Every one of my team members shared my excitement, and we celebrated the success of Operation Barry. It's funny to think that they were so happy for Barry and me. I was just some bloke who'd arrived a couple of months ago, one of many pale-faced foreigners who would come and go in their lifetimes. Yet, even though their home was still ravaged, as they tried to rebuild a life they'd once had, they still showed such genuine happiness for my happiness. For someone like me, an outsider who met a dog.

It's silly to compare situations, or lives, or struggles, but there was something so deeply moving about how Barry could bring us all together. What I saw in my boys when we got him into the car. Even these guys, who knew that Barry might escape this life of danger and turmoil while the truth was that they might never have that chance, they still showed love to Barry and me without any envy or disdain. When I think of the way the people from places like this one are characterised, looked down upon as uncultured or uncivilised, I see that it is the furthest thing from the truth.

'New life for you, Barry!' one of my boys blurted out, with a smile beaming from one side of his face to the other.

I held Barry up and made the rounds with the lads, so they all had a chance to say hello to him. Celebrations were in order that night, as it was Thursday, and Thursdays were our drinking night. We were going to toast Barry, our newest team member.

After everyone got their chance to say hello, I tucked him into the fruit-basket-cardboard-box-bed-thing and placed it in the back of our Land Cruiser. Not a minute after I hit the ignition he was snoring away loudly. He was completely zonked out, slept right through the two-hour journey, and he stayed out cold even when we arrived. I doubt he'd had a genuinely relaxed night's rest since his birth, but now he knew he was safe to get some shut-eye. That evening, he enjoyed his first night's rest knowing he had nothing to fear. I was going to protect him.

I carried him into my room, placed him gently on the soft duvet on my bed and left him to snore for a little while longer.

'Goodnight Barry,' I said to him.

7

I found myself staring at this dog who snored the heartiest of snores. I wondered what was going through his head, what thoughts filled little Barry's mind. I wondered if he knew what was going on, if he was as excited as I was.

I could listen to him snore all day.

When he woke up, he scanned the room and then his paws felt around as he started to saunter around it. He must have been wondering what on earth this soft floor was.

'That's a carpet, Barry. It's quite nice, isn't it?' The floor of my room provided a considerably less rutted sensation than what Barry had been used to in the great outdoors.

I watched Barry take another step, and another, and another. It was like watching a baby take its first steps. I'd never seen Barry walk before, as he'd always been cooped up in his makeshift home in Raqqa, but he bounced more than he walked; there was a funky syncopation to the way he moved. He loved walking around the carpet, maybe as much as he loved pissing on it.

Barry smelled about as good as you would imagine. I love you, Barry, but when I went in for a kiss that day, I was nearly sick. He reeked of something old that had been left to rot and fester. In Barry's defence, I don't think he'd ever had a shower before, or at least it was safe to assume that he hadn't. You could maybe make the argument that he was showered by the torrential rains that swept through Raqqa that month, but that probably contributed more to the muddy musk that he wore.

Barry did not like showers. He made that abundantly clear.

Human, I do not agree with this, I don't know what you think you're doing but hell no. I suspect if he could speak, he would be saying something along those lines. He was not pleased.

I fireman-carried him into our shower block, where we had a sink with a movable faucet that could act like a tiny showerhead. I placed him inside the basin of the sink, *a perfect fit*, I thought. Barry disagreed. *Not a perfect fit, human.* His four legs split in all directions to stop himself from falling into what he must have believed to be a death trap. At this point Smudge walked in laughing his head off but then lent a hand.

'Come on now, Barry. You need to shower, you smell terrible.' He was impossible to reason with. Even as I threw straight facts at him, he only grew bolder in his defiance, a total affront to the notion of personal hygiene.

He used what little propulsion he could muster with his stubby legs, which, above all, taught him a valuable lesson about his own physical limitations. He did not get very far. And I was very big and strong. I would be disavowed of that confidence later in his life, though, as I learned that dogs eventually grow big and become very strong.

'Calm down, Barry. I'll clean you up, and then we can go see everyone.' I wanted to be stern, but also reassuring. I was still figuring out what kind of parent I wanted to be. *This is really hard*, I thought. My appreciation for my parents was at an all-time high, and this was just getting him showered.

At this point I hadn't even turned the tap on. *He's not going to like this, not one bit*, I thought. I turned the hot water valve 90 degrees clockwise, and out of the faucet sprayed a continuous flow of steamy water.

I held Barry up with one hand and held the faucet like a gun in the other. *You have no power here, Barry*. I was too big, and he was too small, to do anything about it. He was now, completely drenched in water, half his usual size. He was only a wee little thing. He had an annoyed look on his face, but he was beginning to accept the fact that this was happening and there was nothing he could do to stop it.

I got the shampoo, and he knew just from looking at the bottle that he would not like whatever was going to come out of it. He was now kicking water out of the sink, splashing it everywhere. He was cleaning me more effectively than I was cleaning him.

I scrubbed him as best I could. The white foam made him look like a dog dressed as a sheep for Hallowe'en.

I washed away the soap and dried him with a towel.

From start to finish, that lasted about two minutes. Longest. Two. Minutes. Of. My. Life.

This will be a fun regular occurrence, I thought. Although I'd begun strongly considering letting him smell bad. I mean, how bad could it get?

He was super-fluffy after his shower and, more importantly, he smelled wonderful. I did one last check for bites or rashes, but he was completely clean. It was around this time that I discovered Barry wasn't a boy.

Hmm, that's interesting, I thought. *He doesn't appear to have a penis*. It was too late to change the dog's name now, but I knew just the trick to make everything okay.

'She's not Barr-Y,' I said, to no one in particular. 'She's Barr-IE.'

Problem. Solved.

I brought Barrie out to our 'bar'. It was Thursday night, and Thursday nights were when we drank cold cans of crisp Efes beer in our common area. It was decorated with a Kurdish and Syrian flag on one side, and a burnt ISIS flag on the other. On one of the shelves we kept a tommy gun. Anything we found out in Raqqa we'd keep in this room. It was like a little museum of all the trinkets and strange things we found on our excursions to Syria, and on Thursday nights it was the setting for our piss-up.

I introduced Barrie to everyone. She was quite groggy by this point. She'd been through a long day, plus she'd exhausted quite a bit of energy during the battle of the faucet.

Everyone wanted to say hello to her and play with her. She warmed up pretty quickly, falling asleep on at least four different laps throughout the night.

Barrie loved Thursday nights at the bar; it was something to look forward to after a week of work. There are few better ways to decompress than to knock down a couple of cans with some mates.

Harry Cripps, my team leader, was celebrating his birthday one night. It must have been his 120th; the man was as old as time. He'd seen some shit; he'd been with the Royal Navy since the 70s. He didn't do himself any favours with his white stubble and generally grizzled look. He looked like one of those proper old-school sailors. He didn't mind that we took the micky out of him for it.

It was one of the first nights when I really felt like Barrie's dad. She followed me to the bar – she refused to stay alone in the cabin, she hated it. Plus, she enjoyed the attention she got from a room full of people. She ran around, chasing after people's feet, playing with loose string that people would drag around for her entertainment. After a couple of hours, she tired, as did we. We'd had quite a bit to drink. It was a celebration after all.

She dragged herself to me and looked up, to indicate she wanted to be picked up. With the biggest smile, I lumped her onto my lap, and she curled into a comfortable little ball. It reminded me of when I was a kid, back in Dagenham.

We lived in a close-knit community back then, and we had a local pub my dad would bring us to on Sundays, where we'd meet with all the neighbours. The grown-ups would all have a pint or two, while us kids would run around screaming and playing until we were too exhausted to stand.

I'd always seek refuge in the safety of Dad's lap then, and now so did Barrie.

Digger was Barrie's other dad. He was a towering presence and had a strong, defined jaw. He looked like a proper tough Scotsman. He had a talent for arts and crafts; you could tell from his hands that he loved making things. There was this soft side to him – as soon as Barrie walked into the room he turned into a seven-year-old girl.

He was the one in the family who spoiled Barrie. At her welcome party, he presented her with a few gifts that he'd made for her. Somehow, he'd found the time to fashion a small teddy bear from some rope and a pair of old jeans, and he made her a collar, as well as a military harness with her name stitched on to it.

Digger was smitten. He loved dogs. He'd brought back a couple of dogs from Afghanistan with a charity called War Paws and we chatted about them later to try to see if I could take Barrie away from this place.

'Oldman' Andy Jones was her other *other* dad. He was a Welsh veteran. He was from a different generation than most of us there, and you could tell because he operated at a different speed to the rest of us. We used to call him Rockstar Andy. He had more experience in C-IED than most of us combined. He might have had greying hair, but he was more than ready to match Barrie's energy each night, dragging her about as she gnawed on loose pieces of rope and swinging her from side to side like she was a monkey. He really loved her.

I tried to teach Barrie a trick that night. We left the drunken ruckus of the common room for the calm of my bedroom. Barrie was sitting at the foot of my bed looking for some attention. I could barely see her head over it.

'Give me your paw, Barrie. Paw . . . Paw . . . Paw . . .' I tapped my open palm to indicate where she should place her paw, and to my surprise (and delight) she raised her tiny paw and left her soft imprint on my hand. I felt like a proud dad, and I was grinning so much my cheeks hurt. *She's so smart*, I thought. *And so quick*.

Barrie was safe in my arms now, she was my responsibility, my partner in crime.

I went to bed that night feeling as happy as I've ever felt. It was pure happiness, not just for me – everyone wanted to be a part of it.

On her second night with me she was still trying to figure out what a bed was, and where she wanted to sleep. She would spend minutes analysing every square inch of my bedroom, something we would do too, as bomb disposal experts. She found a corner in between my shoes to hide – some survival instincts were hard to shake off. And that's exactly what Barrie was, a survivor.

While the question of where she would sleep was full of uncertainty, the question of where she would pee was all but certain. Absolutely everywhere. I spent the first week just mopping away Barrie's piss. I was starting to reconsider whether she was cute enough for me to be dealing with all of this shit.

'Of course you're worth it,' I said to her. Not that she needed any reassurances; she knew how much I cared for her. We grew closer with each passing day; Barrie and I became inseparable.

You learn a lot about love when you spend twenty minutes each day mopping up dog urine and do it with a smile on your face.

My routine morphed and adapted around Barrie's needs. She was my responsibility and I could feel myself growing into the role. I thought about her all the time, what she needed, what I would do with her, what trick to teach her.

She'd come into the office with me. I remember her inspecting my computer mouse. She'd never seen anything like it before. Was it an animal? What did it do? She'd bounce around it, squaring up, ready to pounce. She did this a lot, and to a lot of objects. She was a fierce little dog, and I never felt safer from the wrath of the computer mouse than when I had Barrie with me.

'Stop attacking the mouse, Barrie, I need it to do my work,' I'd say to her, nervous about raising my voice too much. She always knew how to toe the line between annoying and adorable.

The next moment she'd start attacking the stapler, and then the elusive water bottle. Maybe she thought she was protecting me.

It was amazing to watch this dog, a ball of positivity and love, running about my office. It was hard to believe she was the same dog I'd found whimpering in Raqqa.

I tried to discipline her, but she made me into a big softy. I taught her how to sit in a couple of hours, so she was teachable, but she knew she had us all playing the game by her rules. It was Barrie's world and we were all just living in it.

Andy and Digger loved playing with her. They were always there for her when I couldn't be. If she'd pissed on the floor, they would be the first with a bucket and a mop. And she pissed so much, and so often. I started considering limiting how much water I let her drink. *How important IS hydration?* I began to wonder. I remembered back when she wouldn't even drink a sip of the water I offered her, and now she was essentially 90 per cent water, or at least it seemed that way.

The mood at camp really took an upward turn when Barrie joined the team. She just exuded positivity to everyone. Word spread around that there was a new hot-shot dog in town, and everyone wanted to come and see her and play with her. It was easy to forget we were in Syria when Barrie was around.

Dogs have this remarkable ability to make everything simple. If a dog was around, the most natural progression of events was to pet it. It's like an unwritten contract, or bond, of positivity between you and the dog. And this applied to everyone. From the cooks, to the security detail, to the Syrians, to my bosses.

The following Saturday afternoon, I grouped up five or six of my Syrian boys and explained to them what the offside rule in rugby was. Barrie was at their feet, snooping around.

Already a hilarious premise, but I did seriously try my best. And if you're going to try to explain something as complex as the offside rule, you've got to start at the very beginning. To get a baseline.

'Have you played rugby before?' I looked over to Fareed, my translator, and with a little nod of my head indicated it was important that he relay my question to my boys.

As you might imagine, not many Syrians have ever played rugby. But I was determined to get the knowledge across.

It was a cold day, so I was all snuggled up in this black robe I had over my usual gear, which made me look like a wonderful rugby wizard. And a warm wizard, at that.

'The offside rule is quite tricky,' I continued, 'essentially you cannot have a player be closer to the opponents' goal line than whoever is carrying the ball.' Barrie was barking back and forth by this point, her tail wagging excitedly like windscreen wipers.

The boys came closer, surrounding me on either side in a semicircle. I got a couple of confused nods. The game of rugby is complicated enough, and Fareed was having a hard time himself.

'So, the point of the offside rule is to stop a team from having too much of an advantage from being too forward.'

They shifted even closer, listening intently to my every word, waiting for the translation that would follow.

'If you do gain an advantage from being offside, you give away a penalty.'

They nodded and giggled uncomfortably. I think they understood about as much about the offside rule as Barrie, who was rolling around on the ground. 'Now what she's doing, that's football . . .' I smirked. I'm not sure anyone got the joke, but at least Barrie was having fun.

It was a silly day, one I mostly enjoyed because I got to wear a black robe – remember, folks, Allyness saves lives (this was a common saying between us soldiers, essentially meaning that the functionality of your kit was more important than how it looked) – but it was also a reminder of the wonderful people that are out there fighting in Syria. Always willing to listen, and learn, even if it's just something as inane and utterly useless to them as the offside rule in rugby.

When I left, Barrie followed. She was like my little stalker, always sporting a suspicious look on her face – wherever I went, she followed.

It was crazy how quickly we bonded. I never kept her on a lead when we were in our camp or even out on missions. I loved seeing her run. Her tiny legs always ran at full steam, and the way her ears flapped when she scurried around made her look a little bit like Dumbo. Everything about her made me smile.

Barrie storming into our lives happened in such a short span. Not six days after spotting her for the first time, I already knew I had to set in motion the plan to fly her to the UK. Digger gave me the number for the War Paws charity.

I wasn't sure how I was going to do this, or what exactly 'this' was, but Barrie was coming home with me.

'You're coming home with me,' I said, squishing her between my arms.

8

The next couple of days were overwhelming. Things were progressing so quickly, each day ending more quickly than the last. There was so much to do, and I was confronted with all these new emotions and responsibilities. Barrie shook my life to its very core.

I felt like time was passing so quickly, but I had so much to do. I was still in Syria, in a war zone, doing this incredibly important and dangerous job. I still had to train the guys (who, admittedly, were much easier to train than Barrie) and on top of that I had to take care of Barrie and all of her needs. Plus, all the while I had to find a way to bring Barrie back. An operation I was completely clueless about. I would've struggled to get a dog home from a local RSPCA, let alone from bloody Syria.

There were only so many hours in the day, but I was determined to do all of it. Barrie gave me this jolt of life, a new purpose. I started to feel like perhaps my life didn't have to revolve solely around my identity as a soldier.

When I got back from Raqqa the following week, I sat down and began planning the process to bring Barrie to the

UK. I was on the Facebook page of War Paws, reading through all the different stories of dogs saved from Iraq. My Barrie was going to be a dog just like them.

I sent Louise Hastie a message. She ran War Paws, and was ex-military. She is, to this day, one of my favourite people. She was no-nonsense, and straight to the point. She let me know exactly what was needed, when it was needed and what was going to happen. There was something about her that just inspired confidence.

The more we spoke, the more I realised that nothing fazed her. She was like the Terminator; if there was a stumbling block, she would simply crush her way through it until she got what she wanted. It was incredibly impressive, yet a little frightening at the same time. This was a woman who chose to save dogs in Afghanistan, as a civilian, while a war was still happening out there.

We exchanged a few emails, where I told her all about Barrie. I got all sappy about it, but I'm sure she's used to it. I found out that she had brought hundreds of dogs out of war zones, and it was a passion of hers. The world is a better place because Louise is in it.

Any questions I had she answered, and on the rare occasions she didn't have an answer, she would have it within a day or two.

'You're going to need to raise about £4,500 to get her back to the UK,' she said. 'That will cover costs of fixers, transport, food and accommodation, and all the tests required.'

That seemed doable. She walked me through how to start a GoFundMe page, and said she'd help by sharing it on the charity's page but that I had to spread the word as best I could. Fortunately for me, Barrie already had a little following on Instagram as I'd been documenting Barrie Watch from the very beginning.

Nothing could really start until I raised the necessary funds, so that was the primary focus at the time. Louise told me not to worry about anything else for now.

As with anything I did out there, I sat down to think of a plan. In an ideal situation I'd just post the GoFundMe link on my Facebook, and the world would respond with a shower of love (and money) to bring my dog home. The reality was probably going to be quite a bit different from that.

Barrie was sitting, coiled up next to me, as I dabbled on my laptop. Thinking, thinking, thinking. She was so cute next to me, I just wanted to find a way to show the world just *how* cute she was.

And then it hit me. It was so obvious; it was staring me in the face.

One word: photoshoot.

What better way to show people how cute she was than to show them how cute she was?

I imagined how badass we could look, Barrie and me. I would have all my gear on, looking really serious, maybe hold my gun, and Barrie would be by my side in her vest. It looked so cool in my head. People would see the picture and be compelled to help the cause; I was sure of it.

'People are going to love you, Barrie,' I said to her. She just looked at me blankly, probably just thinking about the next patch of carpet she was going to befoul with her pee that day.

The following morning, I went through the same routine as usual. Barrie and I got up before sunrise, we showered – well, I showered – and we headed for breakfast. As usual, everyone said hi to Barrie, and the chefs offered her a selection of foods. Only the best service for Barrie.

'I think we should do a photoshoot today,' I said to Digger.

'A what?' he responded. Surely he wasn't so old that he didn't know what a photoshoot was?

'A photoshoot. For Barrie. So that we can have some good photos for the GoFundMe page!' I was a little more excited about this than everyone else. I don't think they understood the art that I wanted to create.

'The wee little thing was born a poser,' he said.

He wasn't wrong. After yet another day's work was complete, we sat around near our vehicles. Warm chai tea in our bellies. I felt like a director of photography out there, as I barked instructions.

The sun was blazing. You couldn't have asked for better lighting for the photoshoot. Conditions were perfect.

'We'll get one of Barrie standing here next to me, I'll hold my gun. It'll look good, trust me,' I said to my boys. They started snapping away, and Barrie was set in place. It was as if she knew what she needed to do. It was as if she knew the cameras were on her. She was striking poses.

Everyone was laughing while Barrie was posing. It was like Paris Fashion Week, but sandier.

'Work it, Barrie, work it,' I said to her.

We got a couple of great snaps of her standing by my feet. I stood tall, with my gear on, holding my gun. Just as we planned it. We got another shot where I pointed down to the ground, to instruct her to sit, and she – rather uncharacteristically – was obedient and sat. It was as if she knew we needed to get these pictures as perfect as possible to get her home.

We spent a good half-hour having a laugh, taking various pictures of Barrie and me. At the end, I took my vest and placed it on the ground. I put my gun next to it and took my sunglasses off and hooked them onto one of the pockets. This was my art project. My magnum opus.

I carried Barrie and squeezed her into my vest.

'This is the one.'

She looked so cute. Her paws were sticking out the top, she had this adorable look on her face. No one was going to be able to look at this photo and not feel their heart melting. Not a single person.

Some of the Syrian lads wanted to get involved as well; it looked like it was the most fun they'd had in ages. One of them even volunteered to join the shoot and was trying to look cute next to Barrie.

Before we knew it, it was time for us to head back. Barrie was like this unifying force; she made us all smile, and her energy was contagious.

Late that evening, I fired up my laptop and created the GoFundMe page. It read 'Operation Get Barrie HOME!', with that very photo of Barrie poking out of my vest. The page went live the next day. I shared it on my Facebook, and in less than twenty-four hours we raised over £1,000. This was really happening.

I started freaking out a bit. This was a lot of money, and it felt real for the first time. I'm bringing this dog to the UK. A dog I met here in Syria. I'm not a panicky person, you can't really be panicky when you work around bombs all day, but I was panicking a little . . .

Just a few weeks ago Barrie didn't even exist in my life. Damn.

Life comes at you fast.

Then, it was back to normal again. I had a job to do, I had a routine I followed. I felt like I could just live. I'm not sure if it makes any sense, but in the weeks that followed, I no longer had this lingering stress about what I had to do. Nor were there any riddles or issues I had to solve. I could just wake up each morning with Barrie by my side, get ready for work, take care of her, work out and go to bed each night.

The GoFundMe was still raising money but there wasn't much I could do about that. Louise said she'd sort everything out when the time was right. I was just biding my time, enjoying life with Barrie.

There was a zip about training now that Barrie was with us. She lifted our spirits. When I was working, she always had to be touching me – she'd put her nose on my arm, or she'd lie on me. If I wasn't giving her enough attention, she'd sit on our gear, knowing full well that we'd have to play with her to get her off it.

On our drives in each morning she'd place her head in between the two front seats. She loved watching the world go by. I bet she wondered what awaited her beyond the barren Syrian landscape, what life she was about to embark on.

Each time I looked at Barrie it reminded me of how precious life was. How remarkable it all is, and how your life can change in the course of just a week. Whenever I looked at her, I couldn't imagine a life without her.

9

I've always been prone to making terrible life choices. I could never help it, but I would always wind up being the one who fucked it up. Even simple things, like ordering a Chinese takeaway. Everyone would order without a fuss: spring rolls, chicken chow mein, egg fried rice. And I'd be the idiot who got food poisoning for taking a punt on the menu item no one knew how to pronounce.

That changed when I met Barrie. I knew she was the best decision I'd ever made when I woke up each morning with her by my side. I didn't know to what extent she'd make me and everyone around me better, but I just knew she would. She was a little mongrel who pissed everywhere, but she was my little mongrel who pissed everywhere.

No one was happier about me finding Barrie than my friend Netty. She was mad about all animals, she wouldn't stop talking about them, but she especially loved dogs. Being the enabler that I am, I would send her pictures of Barrie rolling around, running about, just generally being the cute little diva that she was.

I'd known Netty for three years. She trains with us over at Beyond Limits, and we kept in touch after I moved her to another coach when I decided to go to Syria. She'd text me to make sure I was all right and we'd have casual chats throughout my time out there. I think I needed them, just to remember there was a life back home, with people who actually cared about me.

Every time we'd text, I would send over a typo or misspell a word, and she'd always kick off.

'How is it that I'm Polish yet I am able to speak English better than you?'

'*Your* right,' I'd send back, just to piss her off.

Netty was a great friend. Not only did she really care for me, but perhaps, more importantly, she also introduced me to kielbasa sausages. Barrie didn't know this yet, but she'd come to appreciate Netty for those two things as well.

It didn't take long after Netty saw a picture of Barrie for her to decide that she was going to be her mum. I don't believe I was really consulted on the decision, and I don't think I would have been allowed to veto, but I didn't mind it. Not one bit.

'I can't believe it, I really can't,' she said. Truthfully, I don't think I was fully aware of what I'd done either.

'We'll raise her, you and me,' I replied, adding, 'I hope you're ready to potty-train her, because I sure as hell don't think I'll ever be able to.'

Netty was the big equaliser I needed in life. She knew when to give me a stern telling-off, but she always knew when I needed to be pulled out of my own thoughts. Lassoed away from that dark place. But little did I know we would end up together.

I think she was proud of me, because Netty loves dogs more than she loves humans. Her being proud made me feel proud of myself. It was the first time I'd really been proud of something I'd done that wasn't strictly a military accomplishment.

While I was away on jobs, often with Barrie trotting by my side, Netty was back home in Essex planning out our lives as parents. She was organised, and that's probably the understatement of the year.

She's the kind of person who is always at the airport four or five hours before her flight, 'just in case you have an accident, or something happens on your way to the airport! You never know!' she used to say. I'm sure if she could somehow camp there the night before, she would.

Netty had a way of talking to me that was oddly direct. It must have been a cultural thing, because I never met anyone else who spoke the way she did who wasn't a soldier. She would just talk to me straight. It's something that I've always appreciated in her.

It wasn't just Netty who was excited, I think my mum and dad were too. In those years after Afghanistan, they suffered more than they ever should have. And always in silence.

Back home, I didn't talk to them much. I shut out my own parents. I was a recluse, and I think that hurt them a lot.

Then, to make matters worse, I left for Syria in a hurry, and I didn't really know where my head was at the time. I didn't know if I ever wanted to return to civilian life – or if I could. I'm sure that thought troubled them, too.

With Barrie in the picture, though, it felt natural to talk to them. I would tell them about my day, what Barrie and I were up to. I could let them back into my world again.

One night I told them about the day we had US Navy Seals come into the office.

There were six of them, all massive lads. They looked like they were ready for war and were going to fuck some shit up. They stomped into the office, just towering over everyone.

I remember thinking: *Holy shit, these guys mean business.*

I stood up to greet them, preparing myself for a firm handshake to match their level of sternness, but before I could get to them one of them had spotted Barrie.

'OH. MY. GOD.'

'Is that your puppy?'

'He's so fucking cute. Can I hold him?!'

'It's actually a girl,' I said, smugly, as if only an idiot would think she was a boy. 'Of course you can.'

One of the lads took her. Barrie was always a willing participant when it came to cuddles, and he cradled her in his arms.

Each day with her was like that, I'd tell Mum and Dad. She just softened everyone up. Mum was always happy to hear a story about Barrie.

'Get her back as soon as you can,' she'd say, hinting that I should head back soon, too. 'I hope Toby will be all right with all of this.'

Toby, our Yorkshire terrier, was old and grumpy, and definitely would not have been all right with the introduction of a new sibling. *You can't satisfy everyone,* I thought.

Whenever I got back from a day out in Raqqa, I'd look forward to Netty's texts. She'd always impatiently ask me about Barrie, and about my day.

We would spend hours just chatting about where we'd take Barrie for walks. Belhus Park, Grays Beach Riverside Park, Thorndon Country Park. All the dogs would want to befriend her, and maybe she would even find herself a boyfriend.

'Okay now, Sean, don't get ahead of yourself.'

As I said, I needed Netty to keep me grounded.

We Skyped sometimes. It was always funny to me how Netty would be beaming with joy and without fail I'd always think at first that it was because she wanted to talk to me, when in reality she just wanted to see what Barrie was up to.

'Where is she? Let me see her!' she'd demand. It's amazing how with just our phones a dog in Syria can bark at a woman in a gym in Essex, and that's what Barrie did. I'd have to hold the phone facing this dog who had not a clue of Netty's existence or of what a phone was, and allow them to have this nonsensical conversation with each other.

'How are you doing, Barrie?' she'd ask.

It didn't matter what Barrie did, Netty always took it as a direct response to her questions. I can't mock Netty too much for how she interacted with Barrie, as I was exactly the same.

It was oddly warming to the heart to see Netty interact with this dog she'd never met. She was so invested in Barrie, and she was so motivated for this little life we were planning to carve out for ourselves. Netty and I had been good friends already, but there was a new solidity to our relationship now, because of Barrie.

Barrie was like that, really, she brought people together. Loneliness was a long-lost feeling, because it wasn't just her company – she would bring the company of others. One night I was Skyping with Netty. We were discussing a couple of things about Beyond Limits, something we did quite frequently. She was quickly becoming my sort of adviser, the little angel on my shoulder letting me know what to do. That evening, I could hear footsteps nearing from the corridor outside my door.

My cabin was near where the Syrians stayed, and I always left my door open for anyone to pop by. But truth be told, no one ever popped by before. Now, though, there was more foot traffic outside my room than ever before. Maybe they were really interested in the many lessons I had to offer in life, *just maybe.*

I looked up when the steps grew louder and it became clear that they'd stopped just outside my cabin. I could see the faint shadow of two feet in the gap below the door. They knocked. It turned out to be one of my Syrian boys.

They always wanted to play with Barrie. This became something of a nightly occurrence; people would pop by to see how she was doing. Netty made sure to make it clear to me that the slot of Barrie's mum had already been filled, and that any potential suitors should be warned of that fact.

Netty and I would talk about our plans together, and it felt like we'd skipped a whole part of our relationship that would normally precede this, but that's how it was. There was no real lead-up to it all, but suddenly we were thick as thieves. It was all happening before we had any time to realise exactly what 'it' was.

It's funny, because we were growing so close and the reality that we were going to be Barrie's parents became so concrete before any real plans to bring Barrie back had ever been realised. I guess it felt nice to be making plans with someone back home. It felt like there was something real to look forward to.

I was excited about going back to being a civilian, something I had been afraid I'd never feel again. It had been a long time since I felt happy about anything to do with my future; for a while, it had felt like nothing good could ever happen for me.

I lay on my bed and thought about that plan I had as a twenty-year-old, to have a family of my own. I thought about Nic, and how I'd messed that all up. I thought about being a dad, how close I was to the highest of highs and how I'd wound up in the darkest of days.

'That wasn't even that long ago,' I muttered to myself. It still sent shivers down my spine. A mix of disappointment, sadness and anger always filled me when I remembered those days. In myself, in the world, in everything.

Barrie was on her back with her paws lifted in the air, her head tilted to the side. She was smiling.

'You're my family,' I said to her. She was my family. Little did I know that this little thing would bring me and Netty together and make the life I wanted. It wasn't exactly the way I'd thought it out in my head, but that plan went tits-up almost as quickly as it was formed. Unconventional paths brought us all together, and we were going to be an unconventional family.

10

A day, a mood, can change in an instant in Syria.

We were still reeling from Barrie's sudden arrival, and we tried to carry the positive momentum forward into our jobs in Raqqa. On the morning of 14 March, we were all having a laugh. Barrie was literally barking orders; she'd taken a supervisory role into her own paws.

We spent most of our morning sweeping through a mass grave, where we'd found piles of bodies dumped on top of each other. I felt a gelid breeze fizzle through me that morning. We could see fingers poking through the earth, fingers small enough to have been those of children. It was a harrowing walk.

We were there on a job, but it was impossible to escape that feeling of disquiet while walking through it. These people were all tortured before being thrown in here like animals. They had families and friends, who were never allowed to mourn them. We stood there, just for a second, to pay our respects.

There was a strong stench of death. It was thick, you could almost feel it with your hands.

'This isn't right,' I muttered to myself. It simply wasn't. Who knows what lives these people could've lived, what experiences they could have had? These were people, human beings. Yet all that was left of them was rotting flesh and bones, crawling with maggots and God knows what else. I wondered if anyone missed them or remembered them. If their memory died with them in these graves, lumped on top of hundreds of unnamed victims.

When you've spent a couple of hours in that environment, you need to shake it off. We tried to lighten the mood up a bit after that. I hadn't managed to fit in my morning workout that day, so instead I decided to pick up one of my Syrian boys to do some squats. He must have weighed about 60 kilos, and factoring in 15 kilos for the gear, it was a legitimate workout.

I went up and down, up and down. He started crying in fits of laughter. We needed to be silly every now and then, if we didn't want to go mad.

Then, in the distance, we saw puffs of dust forming. It was a small convoy of cars heading in our direction. Syrian Defence Force (SDF). They were the good guys.

They told Fareed that they were going to go and search this olive grove that was situated less than a kilometre south-east from where we were.

Olive groves were not a fun place to hang out. My first olive grove experience was quite memorable; it was my first week in Syria and I found about seventeen IEDs scattered across it. That wasn't the memorable part, although seventeen IEDs is a hell of a lot; there was this mad geezer who was farming when we got there, and he continued to farm long after we left.

We'd been working on this area for a couple of weeks by now, so I asked Fareed to tell them that I'd interviewed a man in his home on Monday, who'd told me that this olive grove was full of IEDs. He said that four or five children had died there in the past month.

Fareed tried to dissuade them from going but there was nothing we could do. I even showed them a video I'd taken of the interview, but they insisted that they needed to go in. They'd been given orders to investigate the olive grove, and we had no authority to stop them.

They made entry into the olive grove, and about an hour later there was a massive explosion. At first we could see the eruption of smoke shoot into the sky, and then a second later we heard it.

We were trained for situations such as this one, we had set routines we practised time and time again. My team knew what to do. First, we put Barrie in the boot of my vehicle.

'In you go, Barrie,' I said to her, instructing her to sit quietly. 'Be good, I'll be back.'

Everyone else packed their kit and got into their respective vehicles. They knew the cars had to be ready to go. We hadn't decided on a course of action yet, but this is what our training is for. It was likely that we'd have to evacuate and get the fuck out of there ASAP.

I sprinted towards the last marked safe point, a road that led to the source of the explosion. Harry Cripps, my team leader, as well as one of our medics and two security guards, ran with me, too.

One of their soldiers yelled out for a medic. There was no way we were going to risk any more lives by entering the olive grove, so we asked them to bring him to us.

It all happened so quickly.

We gave them one of our stretchers to place the casualty on. They carried him arm-in-arm and scrambled to get him on the stretcher and to the safe road. The medic and I began addressing the casualty and the medic immediately tried to stop the bleeding. *Arterial bleeding, it's not looking good.* There was no way we could save this man out here. He needed to be taken to a hospital.

I radioed Fareed, who told everyone to get vehicles ready so that, no matter what we decided to do, we'd be ready to move.

At this point we're focused on getting everyone out of there, the entire area is compromised. At any point there could be an ISIS cell, or a trap, so time was not our friend.

We found out that our injured friend was named Mohammed. Our medic focused on trying to stabilise him, but his face was completely messed up. Blood was gushing everywhere. His limbs were all in the wrong places. Our medic frantically wrapped four tourniquets around each severed limb to stop the arterial bleeding.

'We need to get him the fuck out of here.' I looked to Harry, who radioed our camp to inform Mark Buswell of our plan of action. Everyone was in position, everyone was doing their jobs as they were trained to.

The SDF had an ambulance as part of their convoy, and we needed to get Mohammed into the ambulance.

'We need to get him into the ambulance, right fucking now.' I was yelling instructions at the SDF soldier via Fareed. When we reached their ambulance, it was totally empty. No med kit. It was just a car dressed as an ambulance.

'What the fuck is going on?' I looked to Fareed for answers. *This is a joke.* I couldn't believe what I was seeing, or what I wasn't seeing.

Fareed told me they were instructed to bring a medical vehicle with them, so they brought an ambulance with absolutely nothing inside it because they didn't have anything to put inside it. It was absurd, but that was the reality out there. These guys were fighting a never-ending war, but they didn't have the basic tools to survive. They still don't.

We had an ambulance and we took Mohammed, but by this point he'd lost too much blood and he was barely conscious. Our medic kept talking to him, trying to keep him awake.

There were three steps we had to follow to have a chance of saving Mohammed. Stabilise the casualty, get them in the ambulance, get them to the closest hospital.

We barely managed to get Mohammed into our ambulance. I told the SDF soldiers to join our vehicle pack.

My vehicle was at the front, followed by the medical vehicle, team vehicle, then kit vehicle.

There was a US Special Forces base north-west from our location, roughly twelve kilometres away, which was the closest place I was happy to take him to. There was another hospital a similar distance away, but I knew the American Special Forces surgeons were better than your everyday Syrian medics, and they were probably better equipped to deal with this, too. I made the decision, radioed Mark, and we set off. They were now contacting the base to let them know we were coming.

Six and a half minutes. That's the time between hearing the explosion and when we drove off. It all happened in a flash.

Raqqa was a busy city. We had to weave our way through traffic, potholes, roads that no longer were roads, as quickly as possible without any sirens or lights.

Our Land Cruisers jounced through the furrowed streets of Raqqa, slaloming between civilian cars that were being instructed to move aside by the frantic flailing of arms from our vehicles.

As we arrived at the base we stopped all the vehicles on the road very abruptly. I jumped out of my car and onto the bonnet of the ambulance and instructed them to drive to the gates.

We just about made it.

The guard threw the gate open and I started sprinting in front of the ambulance to get to the doctors first and give them a fighting chance to get themselves ready for Mohammed. My security guard sprinted with me. He was like my shadow – wherever I went, he went. I'd written a 9 Line report, the standardised report for casualties, so they could prepare for what was coming.

They took Mohammed and at that point everything went quiet. The adrenaline began to wear off. It was just us and the SDF soldiers and we didn't know each other's names, we couldn't really communicate with each other; all we knew was that we'd just gone through hell and back together.

One Syrian soldier fainted. The events of the day had worn him out.

We all stood outside the surgery, waiting together. The hospital wasn't really a hospital, it was a dishevelled house whose walls weren't even painted. The operating theatre would have been someone's living room. But out here, this was the best there was.

Now that we'd done all that we could possibly do, I could start checking on my boys. The period after is the most difficult, because you keep replaying the events over and over again. I checked with the medic first. He was completely drenched in another man's blood, and I needed him to know he'd done a top job. He said he was okay. So were the rest of my boys. Barrie, too, she was fine.

After about ten minutes we drove back to our base.

The drive back was heavy, because you can't help but think about what's just happened, and what you could have done better. I'd been communicating with Mark and Harry throughout our journey back, recounting the events as I saw them. Each decision, each reaction, each result.

This was normal. Out there, we had to document everything we did. The details of the events were crucial. You had to see it as black and white.

When we reached our base in Tabqah, we parked our cars and took the ambulance to the wash point, where we cleaned it of all the blood. We stood around in silence, spraying the back of the ambulance with a hose, and then swept the blood away with brooms.

All this blood, I thought. *All this blood was flowing in a man's body just a couple of hours ago.* Now, the blood was being washed away into drains.

Harry and I briefed Mark on what had happened, then got to writing our reports for the day, as best we could. Even on nights like that, you had to be clear and lucid. We were team leaders, so we couldn't allow ourselves to be emotional about what had happened.

We have a set way of doing things in the military. 'My job, my kit, our kit, my team, then me.' That was the order of importance, so I had to make sure the job was done, that our kit was sorted and cleaned, that my team was all right, and then I could see to myself.

Everyone hit the showers after that. No one spoke; not one sound could be heard, except for the steady burble of running water pouring down our bodies. The shower floors were stained a deep crimson. *It's always worse to wash off someone else's blood than your own.*

At six that evening I got called into Mark's office. I knew then that Mohammed didn't make it.

We learned that Mohammed was a tough motherfucker. He was a bomb disposal expert, he was one of us, and he'd survived a bomb before. Lost an eye in the process.

I called my team into our common room, and we sat around a table. My job now was to make sure everyone was okay, and that they knew they'd done a tremendous job.

'It's been a long and difficult day,' I said to them. 'It's not the outcome we wanted, but I'm proud of all of you.'

It was the truth, but it didn't make it any easier.

I let them know Mohammed didn't make it. 'We did everything we possibly could, we trained well, we were quick on the scene. We did everything we could.'

We had to shake it off, shove those dark feelings deep in the box. Most of us went to the gym for a late-night work-out. I brought Barrie with me. She was always happy, and that made me happy.

On nights like those, the workouts were incredibly intense. You just keep pushing, pushing, pushing. The gym was my sanctuary, it was where I could block out the world, tire myself out to the point where I couldn't think. I felt a deep red anger that night.

One. Two. Three. Four. Five. Six. Seven. Eight.

I did repetition after repetition, lifting heavier and heavier weights.

One. Two. Three. Four. Five. Six. Seven. Eight.

Each time I lifted the barbell up in the air I felt strong, like there wasn't any weight I couldn't carry.

One. Two. Three. Four. Five. Six. Seven. Eight.

I let out a massive breath. Barrie was sitting quietly next to the bench I was sat on. *She looks so peaceful*, I thought. I let out another massive breath. By now, my tank top was heavy and drenched in sweat.

One. Two. Three. Four. Five. Six. Seven. Eight.

The barbell clanked onto the stand as I finished my final rep. I sat for a moment on the bench, feeling exhausted. Exhausted from the workout, exhausted from everything really.

Back in my bedroom I was thankful I had Barrie with me. Over in Syria, it wasn't like back in the army where we'd sleep in tents or barracks with all the boys. Here you were completely isolated. On days like the one we'd all just experienced, it felt especially lonely.

Things were different now with Barrie. I could talk to her and play with her. I took care of her, but she took care of me too.

She made me feel like everything was going to be okay.

'Today was rough, Barrie.'

Mohammed and I were completely different people, from different backgrounds, who lived different lives. Yet, we were one and the same.

Rest in peace, you mad bastard. That night, like most nights, I tried to shut it all away.

On the floor, Barrie had only one thought on her mind: cuddles. She looked at me. She was upside down on her back, her paws raised in the air as if to ask me to hold her. I carried her slender body in my arms and felt the weight of the world lift off my shoulders.

11

Barrie woke me up each morning by sitting on my face. She would crawl up onto my chest and tread up and down until I eventually abandoned my will to sleep.

The days that followed Mohammed's death felt colder than usual. The Syrian winter was yet to relinquish its reign to the looming spring sprightliness.

Moving on from Mohammed was difficult and uncomfortable, but we had to move on. If we didn't, we risked opening the floodgates for thoughts that none of us were equipped to handle. On top of that, we had a responsibility, and a job to do, and that didn't end with his final heartbeat. It sounds cold, but out there this was the reality of it. Most days were uneventful, but the risk was always there. Raqqa didn't stop being Raqqa overnight.

Our drive into the city was much the same as it always was. Barrie was in her favourite spot, wedged between the two front seats, so she could watch the world pass by.

Everything was the same that morning. I brushed my teeth like I always did, showered, briefed my team. We drove in the same car, set up our chai tea stand like we always did, and we searched for IEDs around Raqqa. Everything was the same, yet everything had changed. None of us had known Mohammed, but we all felt deeply connected with him.

Working made it easier to forget. When you're clearing potentially life-ending bombs, you're immediately locked back into that mindset where nothing else really matters. It's just you and the IED. The structure, the systems in place, they allowed us to do our jobs. It helped that doing our jobs well was our best chance of not dying.

We were trained to function in this way. I remembered my training as a fresh-faced teen, how everything from the way I cleaned my boots, to the way I stood, to the way I spoke, was heavily scrutinised. It had to be perfect, and I had to be disciplined. Nothing else mattered.

It's in the moments when we're left to our own devices, without the distraction of our jobs, when life becomes an inescapable hell. In those moments, Barrie was like a peppy source of joy.

That morning, Digger unravelled a stout hempen rope he'd brought with him. It must have been thirty metres long. He slung it round the back of our vehicle and tied it to the tow bar.

'We'll tie you right here, nice and secure,' he said to Barrie. 'This way you can run around and we don't need to worry about you too much.'

We took turns throughout the morning to play with Barrie. She was our little escape, like a portal into a different place from where we were.

It seems silly, but none of us ever spoke about how Mohammed's death affected us. We were soldiers, we didn't do that kind of thing. We're trained to block those emotions out, and most of us lived in denial of the atrocities that we witnessed.

Barrie allowed us to cope, helped us to cope, without ever having to speak about it.

As the sun began setting on the Syrian skyline, we had finished clearing a school of IEDs. With all that was happening, successfully clearing the school was a wonderful feeling. Knowing that we'd made a small sliver of Raqqa safer for its civilians was a reminder of why we were out there, and why it was worth it. It was a mixed bag, as we knew that even with all the work we were putting in to make these areas safe, this school would probably never be full of pupils again. But we had to find positivity wherever we could.

After what had been a long day, I untied Barrie and she leapt into my arms. I carried her back into the school we'd just cleared, walking her through the corridors where, at a different time, students would have shuffled around to get to their classes. In one classroom, the front half of the desks and chairs were still organised in orderly rows, while the back half of the classroom simply didn't exist. This fourth-floor classroom had been blown open by bombs and was now a lookout overseeing all of Raqqa. The Syrian skyline wasn't New York, but it was bizarrely beautiful watching the sun set that evening with Barrie in my arms.

'This was once a city, Barrie, a city like London where you'll be very soon. It wasn't always like this,' I said to her.

We continued our wander through the school. There were hundreds of holes perforating each wall.

'These are gunshot holes,' I said to her. 'Children used to come here to learn before all hell broke loose with the war.'

Standing in that school filled me with a deep sadness. Something terrible had unfolded here. I imagined the terrified screams of children cowering behind the few walls that still stood to protect them, as gunshots sprayed violently across. And somehow, we had to just move on from it. It was one building of thousands. A checklist that we had to go through. We had to pretend that this was all normal.

I held Barrie tightly in my arms. I wanted to keep her safe from all of this. It was my duty to get her away from this devastation, from this place devoid of life.

'A new life for Barrie' – that's what one of my Syrian boys said the day we brought her back, and it was something I was determined to do. For the two of us.

I shook it off. I couldn't let myself think those things, I couldn't afford to.

We turned round and made our way back to our vehicles, where my team was relaxing on plastic chairs, enjoying cups of warm chai. Barrie sprang out of my arms and began attacking the unsuspecting legs that dangled within her reach.

'You're going to be a problem when you get big, aren't ya?' said Digger, as an unrelenting Barrie attempted to boost herself onto his lap. Her legs were too small to make the jump, but Digger caught her in mid-air and stuck the landing for her.

Wherever Barrie was, laughter followed. It didn't matter where we were, or what we were doing; if you caught a glimpse of her, a grin would quickly form on your face.

On our journeys back to Tabqah, Barrie would pass out almost instantly. Something about the bumpy ride back to camp made the perfect setting for her to start snoozing away. Harry and I would laugh, because she would snore so vociferously we wondered if perhaps she had a future as an opera singer.

I took advantage of how large our compound was to take Barrie for long walks around the perimeter fence. We'd go three or four times round, some evenings. It's no secret that dogs need to be walked, but I think I needed those walks just as much as, if not more than, she did. We used to talk a lot. I'd do most of the talking.

'It won't always be like this,' I'd say to her. 'You'll be in a different country, with massive parks, and very little rubble.'

I could speak to Barrie about anything. It felt like having my therapist Kim with me, only much cuter. *Kim, if you ever read this, you're cute too.*

Barrie could fuel a small town with the energy she always seemed to have. There was never a corner in a room she didn't feel compelled to inspect, not a toy she didn't want to play with. If there was a person in sight, she would hurtle her tiny body towards them and demand attention.

Taking care of her was a full-time gig. She was a tireless little monkey, who needed to be played with, washed (and we know what a thankless ordeal that is), fed and trained.

I had to write a daily report, which was usually a menial task, but Barrie always made it fun. She enjoyed annoying me; often she'd be pootling across my keyboard as I tried to type. Any attempts to push her aside were met with aversion.

'Barrie!' I'd mutter, a faint attempt to be stern. 'I've got to write this report. Once I'm done, we can go play, okay?'

Barrie was a master negotiator. I don't know why I even tried.

She always ignored my pleas, and the moment she realised I wasn't going to let her walk all over me (or my keyboard), she would sit on it in defiance, maintaining eye contact the whole while.

Behind her, on my computer screen, I could see new lines forming in my report.

ASAFDDSAGGHDGDGHSGGHJAHDHGJDHSAGDHS AGJDGSJHSAHHSDHSJAGDHJHJHHSHJHDSAGHJDHA SGHDHJSAGDHJSAGDHJGSAHJDGSHJAGDJHSAGDJSA HJGDHJSAGDHJGSAGHDJGSAHJDGSADHJSAGSDA GHDGASHJDHJ

'Goddammit, Barrie.'

Everyone laughed at my struggles. Barrie loved every bit of it. She knew exactly what she was doing. Once the damage was done, she'd walk off as if she never really wanted to walk on my keyboard anyway. *That's a power move*, I'd think.

If I put her on the floor, she'd make her way around the room to say hello to everyone in the office. When she wasn't busy pissing everywhere, she was actually very polite and well-mannered.

To the surprise of no one, Barrie's favourite time of the day was breakfast time. I've heard that breakfast is supposedly the most important meal of the day, and she took that to heart. She ate all the damn time, in fact. I began to worry that I'd brought back a pig that had disguised itself as a dog.

There was a feeling in the camp that everyone wanted to be a part of Barrie's life, that they wanted to make sure she felt at home. She was a spoilt little dog. The kitchen staff were especially guilty of spoiling her; they would always anticipate her arrival in the mornings. It was as if royalty had entered the premises when she walked into the kitchen.

We had Malaysian chefs who cooked the most amazing food. In the morning, they would reserve a special plate for Barrie with a host of delicacies that they prepared expressly for her. Grilled chicken was her favourite. It was always funny to watch the chefs squeal when they saw her; she always brought out a childlike giddiness in people.

Throughout my day, people would stop me to ask me about Barrie. The first thing out of anyone's mouth if we bumped into each other was, 'Where is Barrie?' or 'How is Barrie?' People kept biscuits with them just in case Barrie would be there, so they could feed her.

Caring for Barrie was quickly becoming a big part of my identity; for the first time I was more than just a soldier.

SEAN LAIDLAW

Each night I took her out for walks, made sure she was fed, made sure she felt loved. Being a dog's dad was something I'd never anticipated, nor was it something I'd have thought I'd be able to do. But it did reveal in me a desire to be better, for Barrie. I'd lived selfishly for a long time, concerned just with what I needed to do, and I was so overwhelmed with dealing with my own issues that I often neglected those around me.

Caring for Barrie made me better. In many ways she was caring for me too, nurturing me and forcing me to mature as a person. Netty and I would speak for hours at night, forming concrete plans for us three in Essex. We thought about accommodation, about work, how we'd balance our commitments. We felt like grown-ups.

I felt good about myself. Here was this dog who trusted no one, who chose to trust me. The way she always looked for me, it made me feel like I was a good person. She didn't see me as a failure, or a fuck-up, she just loved me.

For so long I'd believed I was this terrible person, and all my decisions at the time had seemed to reflect that.

I often thought about the day I found her. I remember how lonely she looked, and how lonely I felt. Seeing her each day, how normal it was to have her around, just felt absurd. If we were going to be lonely, we would be lonely together.

With each passing day, we grew closer and more inseparable. Our routine was perfect. We woke up together, we ate breakfast together, we even worked together. If I couldn't be with her, one of the boys was always happy to take care of her. At night, after a long and gruelling day of work, there was no greater feeling than to be welcomed by a beaming Barrie, who always had a smile on her face.

I couldn't wait to bring Barrie home with me.

12

In late March I took a few weeks out of Syria to spend back home in Essex. One of my best mates, David Rawlings, was getting married, and I had the honour of being best man.

It was nice to get some time away from Syria, especially since I now had a little more solidity in my life with Barrie around. I wasn't shuffling about nervously, with cluttered thoughts clouding my mind. I could be back and enjoy life. It was strange – I had no worries.

Well, one worry, as my journey back home required me to first cross that damned death river once again. The Tigris. I hoped, maybe naively, that in the months I'd been in Syria someone would have built a normal, safe and sturdy bridge.

They hadn't.

It was terrifying.

Someone, anyone, please build a bridge there.

Other than the death bridge, my journey back to Essex went without a hitch. After about a day, I was back in London, far away from sand, dunes and Land Cruisers.

Essex was cold, and dark. My parents' home, however, was warm and welcoming. It was unchanged from the last

Barrie, just after we found her and when she came to live on the compound. She revealed a humanity in us all that wasn't always so clear in those parts of the world.

Barrie soon got to know me and the barriers came down completely between us.

Barrie quickly became the talk of the camp and lifted all of our spirits.

'Who is this very cute creature?!'

Making herself right at home in my bed!

I was so nervous waiting for Barrie to come through the doors at the airport – what if she didn't recognise me?

After an anxious few hours the penny dropped for Barrie and she remembered who I was.

The Micra was quite cramped with Barrie in the back – she immediately stuck her head between the seats.

My dad, Ian, is allergic to dog hair but he was instantly smitten with Barrie.

Barrie has proved herself to be very helpful with my work with Beyond Limits…

I'm so lucky to have found this beautiful dog.

Barrie has become a dog influencer and has lots of celebrity dog friends.

If you'd asked me a year ago about holding a birthday party for a dog in a pub I would have thought it was insane.

The party was chaos and completely mad, but totally life-affirming and a whole heap of fun.

Barrie is now a bit too big to be a lap dog!

Always ready for an adventure.

Barrie and Netty have been inseparable since day one.

Barrie is my best friend she's fitted into every single part of my life.

Meeting Barrie was the best day of my life. She didn't know it then, and I'm not sure she knows it now, but she saved me.

A whirlwind of events brought me and Barrie together, and she brought me together with my future wife, Netty.

time I was here. Mum and Dad never liked changing things too much. They were at the door to greet me when I arrived, ecstatic that I was still in one piece, I'm sure, although they were saddened that they couldn't meet Barrie yet.

'When will we get to see her?' asked Mum, while offering me a cup of tea. The first sign that I was well and truly back in England.

'Soon, I think. Depends on when we hit the target.'

'Where is she going to stay?' asked Dad.

'No idea.'

'How is she getting here?' asked Mum.

'No idea . . .'

'What checks does she need to have?' asked Dad.

'No idea . . .'

A pattern was emerging.

'Excited to be back?' asked Dad, remembering that I actually existed.

I was. I truly was. I didn't like being away from Barrie, but I was happy to celebrate my birthday here with family and friends. I was excited to meet Netty, so we could chat about all things Barrie. And David's wedding, of course.

I wasn't worried about Barrie being without me. She was in great hands, namely those of Digger and Andy, who were more than happy to take care of her. They were always so good with her; they loved her every bit as much as I did.

'How is she doing?' I messaged Digger for a quick check-up. I was like a worried mum when their child was away from home for the first time.

'She's one of the best things about being here,' he said.

Digger went on to say that there were times he didn't do any work because time just flew by with Barrie. It brought a smile to my face to hear that. Just the simple fact that Barrie didn't just bring joy into my life, but to so many others, too. So much good could come from just one simple act, one decision. This changed the way I viewed a lot of things; it made me realise that every little choice I made could lead to something good. It made it feel like the things I did could matter, if only to make a single other person smile.

At David's wedding I got to put on my best suit. It had been an age since I'd worn anything but khaki-coloured everything, so I was happy to look fancy for a change. I walked lighter too, swapping my heavy boots for brown Oxfords.

A lot of the people there knew about Barrie, either because someone had told them or because they followed my Instagram. Social media is a funny old thing. Most people asked me how I was doing, but after two or three sentences the questions about Barrie would start flooding in. I didn't mind it at all, I loved talking about her.

'How did you find her?'

'Are you bringing her back?'

'When are you bringing her back?'

'Why is she called Barrie if she's a girl?'

Barrie was the ultimate conversation starter.

'Barrie never let me work. Everything had to revolve around her,' I said to a couple of mates. 'If I was trying to mop up the floor, she'd start attacking the mop hoping I could drag her around. If I was trying to write a report, she'd stick her nose in my face.'

The wedding was a joyous affair; the bride looked beautiful in her pearly white dress. The groom didn't look too shabby himself. We drank a lot of bubbly in extremely posh-looking flutes, and we enjoyed a long evening of celebrations.

I felt normal. No uneasiness, no stress.

I was just happy to be there and enjoyed every moment.

A lot of people were seeing me differently too. We'd be having a chat and people would bring up how amazing it was that I saved this dog, and it was funny, because I never really saw it that way. I just wanted to bring this dog back, because it felt like the right thing to do.

I was in such a good place mentally that I felt good at home. Even if I was just back for a couple of weeks, I don't think I'd ever felt so relaxed. And it was only going to get better when Barrie was here with me.

After the wedding I celebrated my birthday with my family; Mum and Dad noted that I was like a new person compared to the last time I came back from a war zone. My mood was cheerful, and I was better. That's it, no drama.

I blew out my candles, the big 30, and made my wish. I wished for Barrie to be with me, and for everything to be okay. Not great, not amazing, just okay.

Life was good. The wedding, the family, and even the company was doing well. It was such a foreign feeling; I couldn't quite believe it.

Beyond Limits had grown by leaps and bounds while I was in Syria. Not just as a company, but we had a much bigger team, not least thanks to Mitch, who'd been doing so much while I was in Syria. Organising everything and managing the staff and clients. The two of us decided to host a paintball party with the entire team, as a sort of thank-you for all the hard work, but also because it was going to be so much fun to shoot all of them with thousands of paint pellets. They discovered very quickly what a man can do with a gun after a decade in the army. Mitch elected to 'be on shift' at his firehouse for this day, knowing what would happen . . .

I kept myself busy in the last week or so in Essex. It was an opportunity to spend more hours working on Beyond Limits to keep pushing the boundaries of what it could become.

I think Mitch and I were maturing with the company; maturing as people, as trainers and as businessmen. I remember how lost we'd felt when we first started Beyond Limits in 2016. We'd had our very first bootcamp, where we had just two full-time trainers on a big empty field somewhere in Thurrock. Now, we were planning much bigger things.

Mitch and I had long conversations about the philosophy of the company. It was important for us that it reflected our values and our experiences.

When we started Beyond Limits, we did so because we felt we had something unique to offer to people. Not just training them to get fit, not just to lose weight or gain muscle. We were a soldier and a firefighter. Our training taught us discipline, it taught us self-belief and it taught us that we had potential. These were all values we wanted to transmit, but we didn't quite know how to do it.

We introduced a new, intense army bootcamp. It finally hit me that I would probably never be able to escape my military past, as much as I wanted to; the more I tried to run away from it, the more I stumbled. The army bootcamp was a way for me to keep some of what I had as a soldier, but in a civilian setting. We had trenches, and tyres, and obstacle courses. It would be muddy, and exhausting, and there would be loads of yelling. It was going to be exactly like it was in the army, only none of us would be risking our lives.

We'd set routines, for me and for our clients. 'If we can't train ourselves, how could we train others?' Mitch used to say.

'I never want to be in a position where I'm sleeping in my car,' I said to him, after a workout in our gym. 'I'm not doing that again.'

'We won't let that happen, Sean.'

'No drama. No drama.'

I was a different man in 2018. Not disillusioned with what I could be as a civilian, as I was after Afghanistan. Not the man who thought his experiences in the war wouldn't affect him. That I was somehow special. The one soldier who'd escape from the war unscathed and untouched by PTSD. I was vulnerable now, but that made me a better person. I was vulnerable to my emotions, to my deficiencies, to Barrie.

I still had a lot of growing to do, but I was making progress. Progress was all I ever wanted, even back in 2014. I just never realised the progress I really needed to make was related to my mental health.

Everything was slotting into place for my return with Barrie.

I missed her dearly while I was away, but I also got a glimpse into the life we could have. The GoFundMe page was close to hitting its goal, and Netty started getting excited about her newfound motherhood. We were going to see if we could get Barrie back as soon as possible, even if it meant I was still in Syria. Netty didn't hate this idea too much, as it meant she could get some time alone with her.

On 20 April Dad drove me to Heathrow. The end of a much-needed break, but I missed Barrie and was eager to go back to see her. Digger had been sending me updates about her every few days or so, and I couldn't wait to hug her when I got to camp.

My phone began to ring about midway through our journey there. It was from someone from the contractor I was working for. *This can't be good*, I thought.

It wasn't.

The situation in Syria had deteriorated in the weeks I was out. The area was destabilising, and no one was allowed to travel anywhere close to that area. We weren't in Syria as soldiers, so if we got involved in any battles, we would be breaking the law.

Everyone's contracts were being cancelled. I was in shock; I didn't really understand what was happening. I needed to get back to Syria. I couldn't leave Barrie there.

'What do you mean I can't go back to Syria!' I lashed out a bit. It was less of a question than a threat. I just couldn't believe it. 'What's going on?'

We had a routine over in Syria, we had structure. I couldn't believe it was all about to end.

Dad stopped the car at a service station on the M25 and I spoke to three people. First to Matty, to find out what was going on over in Syria.

'It's not good, mate. Everyone is being flown out, and no one is allowed back in,' he said. 'There have been a couple of missile strikes in eastern Syria. We're not sure what's happening.'

Then I messaged Digger.

'What's going on, mate?' I asked.

'We're not too sure, but all of us are leaving ASAP.'

I knew I had to get Barrie out, and I had to get her out right now. By this point, we'd already smashed the £4,500 that Louise had asked for. She was my third phone call.

'Give me an hour,' she said. Louise was like that, she just got shit done. She told me she'd never gotten a dog out of Syria before, but she might know a way to get her out from Erbil.

An hour later, the phone rings, it's Louise.

Our first plan was for someone to drive to our camp and pick her up. Unfortunately, he couldn't make it.

Then she called me again.

'I know someone who will pick her up and take her through the border to Iraq. If you can get Barrie to this location, we can get her out.'

A couple of days later I called Mark Buswell to tell him I needed a massive favour.

'I know it's dangerous and I'm asking a lot of you, but can you get my dog out?' I pleaded to him.

'No bother, Sean, I'll get her there.'

Smuggling a dog out of Syria is a complicated endeavour. I still don't fully understand how it's done or what it entails exactly. But Louise was a machine, and she was determined to save this puppy from Syria and save me from a life without her.

You need to know the right people, who'll do the right thing, on the right day, at the right crossing, at the right time. Louise and I were back and forth all week, we must have contacted over forty people.

She was giving me numbers to call, she was calling people herself. This woman was a godsend. I will never be able to show enough appreciation for everything Louise put into bringing Barrie home, and all she does saving other dogs with War Paws.

About a week later, Mark drove Barrie to the location where the smugglers were supposed to be waiting. I'd never been so anxious before in my life. I was at home pacing around my living room. I was a nervous wreck.

She's going to be okay. She's going to be okay. She's going to be okay. I had to believe she would be.

There was no phone signal outside the camp, so I couldn't contact Mark or Digger to find out what was happening. It was excruciating. The worst feeling was not being there. I felt completely powerless.

Hours later I got a phone call from Mark. I prayed for good news as I picked up.

'Sean,' he said, and then there was a short pause before he said, 'No one was there.'

'Fuck.'

'I'm so sorry, but we couldn't compromise our own safety. We stayed as long as we could.'

I was disappointed, but I understood. Mark was going above and beyond all that I expected of him, and what he was required to do.

Back at camp Digger was still taking care of Barrie. The only solace I could take from all of this was that she was with someone who truly cared for her. If anyone would be there for Barrie through all of this, it was Digger.

Louise called me the following day. She'd got a new driver and a new location. It wasn't her fault the first guy didn't pan out; there were so many risks involved in what we were attempting to do, and it was impossible to predict if someone would turn up or not.

Third time's a charm, I thought.

Mark and Digger took her to the location, and this time they were met by the smuggler. I didn't know this at the time, and my anxiety was shooting through the roof.

Then I got the call. 'They have her. Mission was a success.'

When I heard Mark's voice confirming that Barrie had been successfully taken across the border into Iraq, I felt a massive weight lift off my shoulders. I could breathe again. *They've only gone and fucking done it*. No thank-yous will ever be enough for me to show my gratitude for what they'd done for me, and for Barrie.

War Paws met Barrie in Erbil, in Iraq, where she passed through the same border crossing I had driven through back in January. She was hidden in the back of a truck; she wasn't too conspicuous, but they covered her in some cloth just to be safe. It wasn't really a case of hiding her, more of paying off the border police. Louise sorted all of that out.

I hoped Barrie was feeling all right through all of this. Her world had just changed for the better, she'd barely had time to acclimate to her new life, and now she was alone in a different country. I had to believe she'd trust me to know we were doing what was best for her.

Louise told me that Barrie had to get a passport, get her inoculations done, and go through all the necessary medical checks and vaccinations. At this point she's steering the ship, and I'm just letting her do her thing.

'Whatever you've got to do, do it. I trust you completely,' I said to her.

Barrie had to be brought to a kennels in Jordan, which was recognised by the UK as a quarantine area.

At this point I'm about 90 per cent certain Barrie will be with me. One way or another, she was with War Paws now. It was just a matter of her going through the health check-ups and us figuring out a way to meet her. I knew Louise would find a way. She hadn't given me any reason to doubt it.

There were many people I needed to thank for the success of the mission.

Mark, my boss, who drove Barrie out twice to try to get her out of Syria. Digger and Andy, who took care of her when I was away, and showered her with unconditional love. My teammates: Harry, Johnny, Dave, Smudge, Jeff, Tricky, Simon, Chris and all the Syrian lads who helped with bringing her back and making her feel at home.

This man named Richard, whom I stalked through Instagram to find, who pledged to donate £2,000 to the GoFundMe page. When I sent him a message asking him if he had donated the money, he simply responded with a 'Yeah, hope you have a good life together.' Richard, you're a legend, mate.

Finally, Louise. She was a superstar. None of this would have been possible without her. She was a badass, and someone I have an infinite amount of respect for. Not just for what she did for Barrie and me, but what she continues to do for dogs and soldiers out there. She does it not because she has to, not because she's employed to do so, she simply does it because that's the sort of person she is.

Louise took all the stress away, and even in the two days of utter panic, she absorbed most of the pressure.

I slept easy that night knowing Barrie was in safe hands. She was a step closer to being home.

13

Finding out I wasn't returning to Syria left me shell-shocked. For one, we had to expedite Barrie's rescue, which was already a complicated and stressful operation in and of itself, but it also left me with no time to prepare mentally to be a civilian again. I wasn't ready to go through it all again. I'd made progress since last year, but I still needed more time.

The plan was always to go back to Essex with Barrie, but not like this, and not now. I didn't know if I was ready yet. Less than a year ago I was a complete mess, a wreckage sinking deeper and deeper into a dark abyss, but things were finally looking good for me. I didn't want that to change.

My contract got cancelled, and with it my main source of income. While Beyond Limits was growing, it still wasn't profitable. My personal finances were taking an absolute beating, so to top it all off I had to find a second job. I moved back into my parents' home and had to rethink all of my plans.

I didn't want to let this hiccup stop me in my tracks. No, fuck that. I was going to keep going. What's next? That's all I was thinking.

I had a driving licence that allowed me to drive just about any road vehicle, and in the summer I got hired as an HGV Class 1 driver for a lorry company in Tilbury.

I was really broke, so I worked as much as I could, splitting my time between driving and Beyond Limits. My normal working day would last fifteen hours; sometimes I worked up to eighteen hours running my company from my laptop.

I worried about Barrie, but at the same time she was the motivation I needed to keep pushing myself. All I could think about was how I wanted to still be in Syria with her. I was desperate to be with her.

I was worried about her, but also about myself. *I'm a different person now*. I knew I was. With Barrie I had different responsibilities, I had a different outlook on life. I was Barrie's dad. But I couldn't fight that niggling feeling that it was all about to fall apart. I didn't want to spiral all over again.

I missed her every day.

The sun had yet to set on a sweltering afternoon on 23 July. I wasn't used to the late British sunsets quite yet. I was on my way back to our home depot in Tilbury. I knew it was going to be a shit day as England had lost to New Zealand in the Rugby Sevens final earlier that morning. That, and the fact that I'd been driving since three in the morning, and it was already approaching 5 p.m. I drove towards a roundabout, doing 70, and slowed down to 20 before coming to a stop when I reached the roundabout.

BANG.

Out of nowhere, I heard a massive thud and felt my body jerk forward and back, hitting my face on the steering wheel in the process. *Jesus*. I'd been rear-ended.

I was driving a massive lorry, so if something could make my vehicle move so violently and abruptly, it had to have been a considerable hit. I slammed on the handbrake and jumped out to see what had happened.

My worst fears were realised as I saw the carnage that had erupted behind my lorry. It was bad. Really bad. Why didn't he stop? I couldn't stop asking myself that question, but he hadn't. And there he was, parts of him still in the right places, but most things in the wrong places.

His van was completely crushed and the driver and passenger seat were submerged under the back of my lorry. Bloodied glass shards were littered across the road.

Two motorists who had been a couple of car lengths behind got out of their cars and ran to the scene. As chance would have it, they were an off-duty paramedic and a retired fireman. If there was a group of bystanders that could save this man, it was us.

We were all trained for situations like this. Our instincts kicked in and we started the process of keeping this man alive until the emergency services were at the scene.

I ran to the front of the car and peeled the windscreen off to free his head. The skin on his face was open like a flap. I gently placed it back where it was supposed to be, folding it over to one side.

The medic and fireman, meanwhile, tore the dented door off to gain access to the casualty. The medic then moved in to ensure his cervical spine was still up. I started packing his wounds. He was losing too much blood.

One of his arms, his right one, was detached and required amputation. His ulna and radius popped out of his left forearm. One of his legs had smashed through to the exterior of his car.

There was blood everywhere: on the windscreen, the dashboard, the seats. His face was now a single shade of red. We couldn't move him; the steering wheel had bored into his stomach, and we couldn't risk removing it without him haemorrhaging blood. There wasn't much else we could do but keep him conscious until the emergency services arrived and took him to a hospital.

His legs were pinned in and the front of his car was crushed under the weight of my lorry. It was impossible to determine where his car ended and my lorry started. It was a fucking mess.

I knew time was running out but, as long as he stayed conscious, we stood a chance. I started asking him question after question to keep him awake. I tried to distract him, but he kept asking me if he was going to die. I think he was crying, but I wasn't sure if they were tears or just blood.

'I can't see! I can't see! I can't see!' he yelled, over and over, his voice trembling in fear and agony. He knew he was in trouble. We all did.

'You're okay. This is normal. Don't worry,' I said to him, trying my best to be comforting.

I continued with the barrage of questions to keep his mind active. What's your favourite colour? Favourite food? Where did you grow up? What music do you listen to?

We kept him alive, barely, for about half an hour before the paramedics and fire service got to us.

Now it was out of our hands and we could only watch helplessly as they worked to save the casualty. He'd lost so much blood, each breath he took became more important than the last.

I finally had a chance to look at my lorry. It was completely caved in at the back. I couldn't believe what I was looking at. *Why didn't he stop? Why?*

The sun was beginning to set when I called Mitch. We had a training session later that evening. I let him know I wasn't going to make it, that I'd been in an accident.

'I don't know how long I'll be here for, mate,' I said. He knew this; he was a fireman, so he'd been through this process before.

'Fucking hell, man. You can't seem to catch a break,' he said. I shared his incredulity about the situation. 'How have you left Syria and still have to deal with this shit?'

He was right, I could never seem to catch a break.

It was starting to feel like I wasn't allowed to live a normal life. It didn't seem fair. I started to believe that maybe I brought the battles with me everywhere I went. How could life as a personal trainer and lorry driver make Essex feel like a battlefield, like a goddamned war zone?

A helicopter descended swiftly onto the road. The pilot was an animal, steered through telegraph poles without even flinching, navigating his way down with incredible speed and dexterity.

We saw them take the casualty and place him in the back. I was hopeful he would make it.

The police interviewed us by the side of the road. It was eerie; the casualty had been gone for hours now, but his blood was still moving, pouring out of the car and trickling through the cracks and crevices of the road.

I phoned my boss to let them know what was going on and they contacted their lawyers and did what they needed to do. The police then took my phone, to check if I'd been texting or using WhatsApp at the time of the accident. They drug-tested me as well. This was all normal procedure.

I told them my version of events, which was something I was used to doing. In Syria we documented everything we did, and we wrote detailed reports each day, so this was no different.

At around midnight I was told the man did not make it. I was still standing by the side of the road. There were no sirens wailing any more and there were barely any cars left. Just silence.

The adrenaline was starting to wear off now. I'd gone through the events of the day so many times that I started to blank out. I could either hear all the world's sirens wailing at once, louder and louder, or I heard nothing.

I was cautioned by the police. At this point I just needed to get home and decompress. My boss John came to pick me up. We stopped at a petrol station so I could get a sandwich and a drink. I hadn't eaten all day.

I got to my parents' house just after 1 a.m. They'd waited up for me, but I just wanted to sleep, put this day behind me.

'Are you okay?' they asked.

'Yeah, I'm fine. I'm fine,' I said, I wasn't sure anyone in the room believed it.

I really missed Barrie that night. I hoped to see her when I got to my bedroom. I knew that was impossible, but part of me just hoped that, somehow, she would be there. I'd open the door, and I would see her rolling around. Her tail would be wagging uncontrollably as it always did and she'd growl at me for spending too long away from her. She would square up against me, squinting at me as if to indicate she was about to pounce, and then we'd chase each other round the room. That's how we spent our nights back in Syria. I wanted to be there with her.

I never felt alone with Barrie. That hot summer's night, I felt so alone.

I thought about Mohammed. About all the blood. I thought about how death seemed to follow me around like a ghost, haunting me for something I had done. I was scared I would revert to how I used to be, as I felt hopeless once more. That night, I lay in my bed and I felt my entire body tense up. I was stressed, then I felt anguish, then I felt hot, then cold, and I just wanted to stop feeling all these emotions. I wanted to shut it all out.

The following morning, I woke up and sat on my bed. It wasn't as hot as the day before, but I was drenched in sweat. I took a cold shower, and let the water run on my face for a good fifteen minutes. I chuckled. This would have been Barrie's worst nightmare.

Everyone had gone to work by now.

I knew I had to quit my job. I hated it. I was done with it. I'd suffered a few injuries from the accident, something I'd barely realised through all the commotion. Getting hit so hard, your bones feel like a xylophone that's been thrown at the wall. Physiotherapy wasn't cheap, but I knew I couldn't continue with my job. I decided to take a week off, then work two more weeks before leaving.

I thought of speaking to Kim that day. I didn't know if I was dealing with all of this in the appropriate way. It was so obvious I was reverting to how I'd been the last time. That same feeling of loneliness, of worthlessness. The long hours of work to keep myself far from those thoughts. It was all the same.

I don't know why I couldn't speak to my family about those feelings, but it was just how I'd always dealt with it ever since I joined the military. They were always there for me, but I still felt alone. All the losses in my life, all the death I saw, I always experienced it alone.

It was different with Barrie. She knew when I wanted to talk or when I needed to be distracted. I couldn't quite explain the bond I had with Barrie, but I trusted her completely. Looking back on it, on how I approached my mental health, I think I always feared people would no longer look at me in the same way if they knew of the demons that lurked in my mind. I was scared people would see me as a monster. It seems illogical to me now, but at the time there was little in the way of logic in my life.

I knew I had to be better, for Barrie, because she was going to be with me in just a few months.

I'd made it out of this hole before and I was going to do so again. I couldn't let myself wallow in my own self-hatred, in my own dark thoughts. I couldn't be selfish; Barrie needed more from me. My family needed more from me. I needed more from me.

14

'I better get my shit together,' I muttered to myself. I remember smiling a bit as I said it, because it felt silly. *I'm talking to myself now, am I?* My hands were on the top of my head, with my palms sliding down to cover my eyes. I was a grown man in the foetal position in his parents' living room. *What a bloody mess.*

I hated how quiet things seemed to get. I sat alone on the couch, then I lay down, then I stood up. I was so anxious. I just needed to do something. I was fidgeting so aggressively, I could've pulled the skin right off my fingers. I started breathing in slow, weighty breaths. I needed to expel this sense of dread and anxiety from my brain and body.

It was still only the morning after the accident, but it felt like an eternity had gone by. The breathing helped; if there's one thing the army taught me, it was the ability to calm myself even in troubling situations. Once again, being a soldier was the only thing that brought me any sense of normality. My life was like this massive loop that existed to test the limits of what I could take.

With each breath I sank deeper into the couch; it was comforting, and I allowed myself to feel relaxed, if only for a moment. The fidgeting stopped, but the quiet persisted. I'd catch myself looking at my watch for the time, and the hours kept ticking on, but I remained still, near-catatonic.

Before I knew it, the small hand on my watch hit five and I'd done nothing with my day. That was the motivation to get up; I wasn't the kind of guy to just do nothing. I called Mitch, threw on some gym clothes and headed to the one place I knew I could find some solace.

'Hey man,' I said to him, casual as always. 'I'm headed to the gym now, I'll meet you there.'

The famous British sun reared its blistering head that afternoon, and I was sweating before I'd even lifted a single weight. On my drive into Thurrock, the heat became unbearable, and I had to wind down the windows of my car to allow myself to feel the slight whirl of the oncoming breeze. I looked behind at the empty backseat and imagined my little Barrie sitting there. She loved sitting in the gap between the two front seats, and she'd probably be looking out to the Essex landscape with excitement.

I loved car rides, even in Syria. It was a way of decompressing on the go. It was easy to compartmentalise and organise my thoughts, as you had to focus on driving.

When I got to the gym, Mitch and I just started working out. There was an understanding between us; I think we both worked out whenever we needed to clear our heads. Mitch was probably the one non-soldier who knew what I was going through the most, because just a year ago he'd walked into Grenfell Tower and witnessed that fiery horror first-hand. Some people he saved, some he didn't. I knew that reality far too well.

My mind wandered, as it often did after incidents like this, to my first tour in Afghanistan. When I was with the SBS, just a couple of days before the rescue mission, maybe three or four. It's funny, well not really funny at all, but I'd blocked out this memory for the longest time, and then thinking about Mitch after the car accident all these memories came rushing back.

We used to make ourselves known, the SBS. We would start big, near-theatrical fights in order to flush out where the enemy was, and how many there were. In the villages we raided, we would have people looking out for them while we were engaging in gunfire. The aim was to bug them out – which was a term we used in the army that meant to get them to retreat or run out of position.

When we'd identified where the enemies were staying, we'd wait till nightfall or daybreak and attack those areas.

On one of our missions, we were near the Pakistani border, in the mountains. I remember thinking it was one of the most majestic sights I'd ever seen. I travelled a bit with the army, but it was difficult to really take in the sights when you were at war. There was a beauty to the way the mountains surged, like they were in adulation of the skies above.

We were using a US Black Hawk helicopter with a radar mounted downwards to follow the enemy's vehicles. It was quite ingenious actually; the radar is meant to track metal objects in the air, but when aimed at the ground, it became an incredibly accurate way to track moving vehicles. They would let us know where to go, and the on-land chase would begin. We knew of three smuggle routes from Pakistan into Afghanistan, where the Taliban would bring in IED-making products such as batteries, explosives, wood, wires and anything else they needed.

We stopped by the mountainside and set up camp, propping our tents that were mounted on the backs of our vehicles. We would live there, no questions asked, until new intel came in and we received further instruction.

A few days later we got a shout from the Black Hawk, indicating that an enemy of interest was five clicks out, or five kilometres, so we got our kits on and headed towards them.

When we finally intercepted them, they knew immediately who we were. Our vehicles were hardly inconspicuous; we had a dual-mounted 50-calibre heavy machine gun, and a remote 50-calibre machine gun, which you'd fire with a joystick while sat in a comfy chair in the back of the vehicle. There was an auto-turret function that would allow you to shoot automatically towards gunfire, and there were little screens that would tell you where the shooting came from. When they saw us coming, they knew we meant business.

There was a massive cloud of dust that formed as they fled, but we were close. Very close. In an instant, we caught up to these geezers who were split up in two cars. The adrenaline was bumping at a rate of knots, and I could feel my heart beating like a war drum.

My team stayed back, while one of our vehicles chased the enemy to the left. The second enemy vehicle turned round and attempted to flank us to the right. We opened fire, aiming for its tyres, and the sheer impact of the gunshots caused them to flip over before they could reach us.

'We got them,' I said.

At this point it was pure chaos. The enemy opened fire; all we could hear were AK-47 rounds spraying in our direction, and the reverberations from the shots we were firing back at them. Underneath the deafening sound of bullets hitting reinforced steel, we could hear them screaming. It was angry, like a battle cry. It all happened in a flash, then the gunshots stopped. *BOOM.* Their vehicle exploded. Flames shot into the air, and time stopped for a second.

When the echoes of the fulminations faded, it left their vehicle wrapped in flames that roared high into the sky, burning a hole into the clouds.

Our second vehicle retreated to our position when they heard the blast, leaving the enemy vehicle to escape. When they heard the explosion, the primary focus shifted from chasing the enemy to protecting the team.

I'd never seen anyone burned alive before. I could still hear the screaming, but it wasn't a battle cry any more. It was fear.

Then the screams stopped, replaced by the sound of flesh sizzling and crackling. As I approached their vehicle, the putrid smell of burning flesh was impossible to escape. It was indescribable, nauseating. You can never forget that smell; even thinking about it now I can still feel it lingering in my nose and my mouth.

I was there to search for bombs, so I had to ignore all of that and do my job. I tried to hold my breath in for as long as I could, but that wasn't particularly effective. I knew I had to focus, think about my training, think about what was at stake. The priority was to ensure my team was safe. Everything else was simply noise. I searched the ground nearby; the blaze still engulfed their vehicle and quickly began to blacken it.

When the flames subsided, it revealed a black car, black bodies, black everything. Seeing these people: charred from head to toe, melted flesh, fat that was still burning.

It all came back to me.

I'd not thought about that episode, ever, until today. It sent a shiver down my spine, and suddenly I was restraining this urge to scream and cry. *Focus on the workouts*, I thought. *Just focus, Sean*.

Mitch knew more than most what I was going through; as a fireman he's seen bodies burning, he's heard people's final screams. It was comforting, in a perverse way, to see him persevering and working despite it all. In the gym, we could push it all away, one workout at a time.

I shook my head, put some EDM music on and tried to drown out those feelings. I couldn't let myself fall into that hole again. Mitch had been doing great work with Beyond Limits while I was away in Syria, and this was *our* company. I wasn't going to let us down.

'I really needed that,' I said to Mitch after finishing a gruelling workout. We were drenched in sweat. I decided to head home. I had a lot to think about.

When I got back, I found my parents waiting for me. They both had a look on their faces, a look of concern, that indicated something serious was about to be said.

'We need to talk, Sean,' Dad said, soberly.

'Hi, what's going on?' I replied nonchalantly. I figured it had only been a day since the accident, and they wanted to make sure I was okay. I put on my most casual face to avoid alarming them.

'You're going to want to sit down,' he said. Something *definitely* felt off.

My parents scooted onto the sofa, I sat down on the armchair beside it. Even Toby wiggled his way to the side of my foot. This was a proper family meeting. Mum was holding Dad's hand tightly, gripping it nervously, or worriedly, maybe both.

'No drama,' I said, an attempt to ease them into what was clearly an uncomfortable conversation for them.

'Nothing is confirmed,' he said. My brows furrowed with concern. *What's going on*, I thought. *If he's putting a disclaimer ahead of what he's saying, this can't be good.* 'I'm getting tested for cancer. We don't know if it's anything quite yet, but it's looking quite certain. We're going to do some tests next Mon . . .'

He spoke for a little while longer, but I zoned out. It felt like a bad dream, and I hoped that if I closed my eyes and concentrated hard enough, maybe I'd wake up.

We had a long chat that evening. It was a very Laidlaw conversation. It was direct, very matter-of-fact. I asked him for details, he gave them to the best of his knowledge. We ate dinner, pasta, I think. And that was that.

It had been just over a day since the accident, and I began to wonder what else life was going to throw at me. What more could happen? I felt like I was in a constant struggle for survival. One test after another.

The following week he was referred to Queen's Hospital, in Romford. There, he had an ultrasound, and then a CT scan. I remember they took us into a little room, and after a couple of minutes we were joined by a nurse. She was pleasant and soft-spoken; she went through the checklist of questions that you'd typically get from nurses and let us know more tests were coming. There's an awkwardness to these interactions; we all knew why we were there, but none of us really knew how to react. It felt like a comedy sketch done by people with social anxiety. Then, after a little while, she said it might be the C word, but he'd have to have a biopsy to confirm.

A week later it was confirmed. Liver cancer.

We were at home, watching some telly, when he told me. I looked to Dad; it was clear-cut for me. I just needed solutions.

'What's next?' I asked.

'Not sure, Sean. Chemo, I guess.'

'Can it be operated on?'

'Don't think so.'

'Do you need a liver? Can you use mine? How can I get tested?'

The doctors had already covered that with him, however, and the cancer was situated in an area that couldn't be operated on. I felt helpless, but we were going to figure this out. We were going to fight this cancer together.

At the time my little sister Rachel was eight months pregnant, and we didn't want to do anything to stress her out before the birth, so we didn't tell her about it.

Dad was taking it all on the chin, which wasn't atypical of him, but I was really nervous. All I could think about was how I wanted the cancer to fuck off. I wanted Dad to be healthy.

A couple of weeks later, on 11 August, Dad had his first chemo treatment. It was a Saturday, and there were about ten or twelve people in this large open room. It had a small dividing wall in the shape of a cross in the centre of it. It was quite cold, I remember us both remarking, even though it was blisteringly hot outside that day. The room was dull and monochrome, which, in all honesty, was a little depressing.

We got in at 10 a.m., and were told the whole process

would take about five hours. Dad looked tiny next to me, like he'd already gone through months of chemo. He'd kept the whole cancer thing to himself for a while; I can only imagine under how much stress he'd been.

They hooked him up to a pump with various drugs in it, and a bag with saline to keep him hydrated. They changed the bags every hour. It was very quiet, as you might imagine a room full of patients in a Haematology and Oncology ward would be. It wasn't a joyous scene. Dad and I had normal conversations, just to pass the time.

'I'm looking forward to when you become a stoner,' I said to him, chuckling.

'Oh yeah, you know me. Big on the weed.'

It was a fairly normal morning. We both had the mindset of 'what's next?' Well, we both knew what was next. While all of this was going on Mum was with Rachel at a different hospital in Basildon about fifteen miles away, where she was expecting to give birth any day now. I left Dad at roughly 1 p.m., headed to McDonald's to pick up a bite to eat for them, and drove to Basildon University Hospital. I remember waltzing into her room with a brown bag full of Big Macs and McNuggets thinking this little surprise is going to be the highlight of their day, and when I opened the door, Rachel had her baby girl in her arms.

'She's beautiful,' I said to her, feeling like a proud big brother. Rachel wasn't that annoying little nuisance I grew up with any more; she was going to have her own annoying little nuisance.

'Her name's Sophie,' she said, still flushed from, well, the birth.

Rachel's boyfriend, Michael, stood by her side. Mum looked as delighted as I'd ever seen her. She was wiping away some tears with a small tissue. I, for my part, just felt blissfully happy. My little sister. *My* little sister. A mum. She was going to be the best mother.

I sat on a chair next to Mum, eating this greasy Big Mac, and I knew everything was going to be okay. I looked at my sister, and she was glowing. I looked at little Sophie, at Mum, and they made me feel safe.

A little over an hour later I drove back to see Dad. We sat impatiently as the drugs slowly filled his body.

'When are we getting out of here?' Dad asked impatiently.

'Soon, Dad. Soon.'

Finally, at around 6 p.m., our wishes came true and we could leave. We rushed to Basildon, and Dad got to see his baby niece. He had the most effulgent smile when he held her in his arms for the first time. It was like he'd forgotten all about the cancer.

A day, a mood, can change in an instant.

We were so happy, all of us. No matter what, we had each other. In a way, my family was like my squadron. We protected each other, we fought for each other. Mum even barked orders every now and then.

It was a great day, a happy one. Not just for Rachel or Mum or me, but even for Dad. I saw chemo as a positive thing, as it meant that he was doing what he needed to get better. And he was going to get better, I was sure of it. It was the next step. Rachel and Dad had taken the next step that day, and I wanted to follow suit.

My next step? Get Barrie home.

15

Rachel's daughter wasn't the only good news I received around that time. About a week before Sophie was born, I'd received a little ping on my phone. It was an email from Louise. War Paws had confirmed that Barrie had made the trip from the War Paws kennels in Iraq all the way to Jordan, and Louise put me in contact with a woman named Judith, who was to become my point of contact with my globetrotting little pooch. Or, as I was soon to discover, my not-so-little pooch.

Funnily enough, Barrie had gone through the same crossing into Iraq that I'd gone through, and she was now in Jordan, where I'd spent time during my first years with the British Army. It seemed like fate was bringing us to the same places.

I wasn't too clued up on what exactly was going on; all I knew was that I was going to be reunited with my dog. I just nodded along with what Louise told me. War Paws have saved hundreds of dogs just like Barrie and they knew what they were doing. For the most part, I was just a passenger.

'It'll be at least three months she'll have to be quarantined,' Judith said in her first email. The first of many we'd exchange in the months that followed. 'She'll have to pass a test each month, and after three tests they'll clear her for travel. Then we'll figure out travel arrangements.'

Three months.

That's it. Three months and all the puzzle pieces would fall into place and I'd have Barrie in my arms. In the UK. It still felt surreal to me, each time I thought about it.

I had many questions, many, many, many questions. Above all, I wanted to see how my Barrie was. What she was doing. How she looked. So much had happened since I left Syria, it felt like an eternity had passed since I last saw her.

Judith sent me loads of pictures and videos of Barrie each week, not in the least because I pestered her consistently. I'd be the first to admit it, but I must have been so unbelievably annoying. I'm sure she wouldn't slag me off, but I was messaging her like a desperate ex. I'd characterise myself as being 'very needy'.

One of the pictures she sent me was of Barrie taking a nap – Barrie, much like myself, could sleep anytime and anywhere – and I started tingling all over thinking about how close she was to being with me. I caught myself trying to pet her through my screen on more than one occasion, and sometimes I'd start mumbling to her as if she could hear me. *I'm going mad*, I thought.

Just being able to see her, see how she was doing. It was a massive relief. I was swamped with all kinds of work, but

Barrie always lingered in the back of my mind. There was so much uncertainty with what we were doing; she was still in the Middle East, in a place I'd never been to and didn't really know about. I was clueless about the process, and that was the most difficult part.

I've always had a difficult relationship with not knowing. I didn't like that sensation, I liked certainty. I liked knowing what I was dealing with. Here, I was in a situation I couldn't control, where I couldn't directly affect the outcome. It was hellish, but I trusted Louise and the entire War Paws team.

I took solace in the videos Judith sent me. In one video, Barrie was trotting around this small compound. She'd grown so much since I last saw her, she was nearly unrecognisable. She wasn't round and pudgy any more; she'd grown taller, her legs longer, which gave her an elegance and poise I wasn't used to seeing. *Where's my clumsy Barrie?* I wondered.

Netty was with me as I swiped through the photos. She'd been spending more and more time with me, she said to organise Barrie's arrival, but I think she enjoyed my company. I know I enjoyed having her around. That morning, I was feeling particularly uneasy about whether Barrie would recognise me.

In trying to get Barrie back there was always something that needed to be done, so I had never even stopped to consider that I might be a complete stranger to her, but now I thought about it, it scared me.

Barrie was just a puppy when we met, and our time together was so brief. Realistically, the soonest we'd be reunited would be seven or eight months from the last day I was with her. I did the maths. Okay, Netty did the maths. But Barrie would have gone through so much in her short life by that time; travelling to Iraq and spending months there, then at least three months in Jordan – and that's if everything went swimmingly, and I knew better than to expect that – after which she'd have to travel to the UK. That's a lot of big events, and a lot of them where I wasn't there with her.

'Stop it, of course she'll remember you,' Netty said. She always knew when I was getting into my own head. 'Now focus on what you need to be doing. We have so much we need to organise.'

She was right, as she so often was. The summer months were hectic. Dad was going through chemo, I was working night and day with Mitch on Beyond Limits, and we had to figure out how exactly we were going to accommodate Barrie. Truthfully, it was all a welcome distraction.

'Where is Barrie going to stay?' Netty asked me.

'Good question.'

See, the loose plan – back when I was still under contract – was that when I got back, I would get my own lovely place, and having Barrie wouldn't have been too much of an issue. Maybe we'd find a few landlords who didn't accept pets, and Barrie would still be pissing everywhere, but other than that, it was supposed to be the easiest part of all of this.

That marvellous plan collapsed when the contract got cancelled, one of many things to go awry as a direct consequence of that, as I wound up broke and living with my parents.

Mum and Dad were always supportive of me bringing Barrie back to the UK, from the very moment they saw her cowering in the rubble. 'You have to bring her back with you,' they'd always said, but they, not unlike myself, had expected me to have my own place when I got back.

'Barrie won't be able to stay in the house,' I said to Netty. 'We're going to have to figure something out.'

To add to the ever-growing list of complications that permeated my life, Dad was allergic to fur, and Barrie, as a dog, appeared to have lots of it. We didn't want to risk any triggers or reactions, especially with the chemo, as his immune system was already weakened.

I scratched my head, trying my best to think of a solution. When Netty and I were together we were always able to solve any issues; she was always incredibly logical and prepared with just about anything she did. This was no different. We looked out of the glass sliding door leading to the garden, and outside was a shed. Abandoned and unused since God knows when. It looked like a relic that had survived the Great Fire of London. In this old and dilapidated collection of wood was a potential home for Barrie and me.

'And me . . .' Netty interjected. I think it was at that point that Netty decided to move in with me.

I loved how involved Netty was with the whole process. Just as I couldn't have done anything without Louise, I would've been lost without Netty. There was never any bullshit with Netty, only progress.

We were standing outside, staring at this broken-down shed. Some light managed to sneak through the tree leaves, revealing cobwebs that swept across every corner of the old wood. It looked like the setting of scary ghost tales, not so much a quaint home for a man and his dog.

It took a bit of imagination, but there was potential there.

A lot of work was required, a lot being a massive under-statement. Parts of the walls were begging to be torn down, and the wood looked like it would be better placed on a stack to be lit for a barbecue. There wasn't a proper toilet or shower – which would probably have been ideal for Barrie – and no bed, or anything. It was something, though, better than nothing. It was a solution. And let's be honest, who didn't dream of living in a shed in their parents' back garden when they were thirty? This guy certainly did.

Netty and I continued to inspect the shed. We felt like architects and engineers for an afternoon. Outside, on a wooden deck, was the most out-of-place hot tub you could ever find. We used it a lot when we moved in but it has been collecting dust for a while.'

'Chalet with an en suite Jacuzzi,' I said to Netty, raising my eyebrows in a sexy fashion, or at least what I thought to be sexy. I just wanted to show off my French.

'Yeah, *chalet*. Sure thing, Sean.'

It didn't look too bad inside. There was space for a bed, room for Barrie to trot about like she always did. It reminded me a lot of the different containers I'd slept in while in Syria and Iraq.

'Here!' I proclaimed loudly. 'Here, we'll have our TV!'

Netty just stared at me blankly, rolling her eyes.

'We would have a shower in here,' I said, pointing at an empty space to the left of the shed. 'And a toilet here. It'll be great.'

And Netty said, 'Here the sofa will go and I can go here too!'

It was fun to imagine this place being completely different. It could be cosy and, while far from being ideal, it would be a home. I think I'd abandoned the notion of things being 'ideal' a long time ago; life had different plans for me, and I had to go with the flow. And the flow was saying this was our home.

We were still months away from Barrie coming over, but Netty was always on my case to make sure I was making progress with everything that I had to do. She was an assiduous planner, constantly pestering me about everything. It was cute.

We exited the shed and took one more look at it. I felt like we were having a moment; I had my arms wrapped around her shoulders, and the sun was setting. Okay, the sun wasn't setting, it was still the morning, but everything sounds better if it happens while the sun is setting.

'This will be our home,' I said, all starry-eyed.

'Yeah, but don't forget all the work you have to do.'

I guess we weren't really having a moment at all.

16

Soon after, summer was over, replaced by cool mornings and early evenings. The streets were now covered in red and yellow leaves that peppered the ground, rustling along to wherever the cold winds chose to carry them. I don't normally enjoy autumn, but I welcomed this one with open arms, even with all its gloom, and the rain it brought with it. I wanted summer to be over, I needed it to be in the past.

Work kept me busy, maybe too busy, but I needed that stimulus. So much was happening all at once, I barely even had time to realise that it had been months since the accident. My niece, little Sophie, had begun grabbing things, and had a little patch of hair growing at the top of her head. Dad's chemo was progressing well. Barrie, too, was just one successful test away from getting the green light to travel to the UK. I wondered where all the time had gone.

After that tempestuous summer, I couldn't escape the feeling of fear that I might spiral again. I didn't know how I'd react; I barely knew what was going on back in 2014. All I truly remembered was the dread, and how lethargic I felt, and that coping with how quickly time was passing was an impossible feeling that made me shirk all my responsibilities.

Now, time was passing quickly too. But it was different. There was so much to do, but there was an eagerness to do it all. Things weren't looking bleak at all – quite the opposite. Beyond Limits was now my full-time job, and it allowed me to start a new routine, one that was compatible with civilian life.

Each day was the same. I woke up, early, always before sunrise. Even when it felt so cold that I didn't want to leave the warmth of my bed, I forced myself up. Same time each morning. Workout. Shower. Tea with Mum and Dad, then off to the gym.

That box I used to shove everything in? I binned it. Kim's words resonated with me more than ever; I let myself feel everything I had to feel.

Dad was getting better. He was reacting well to the treatment; he looked healthier than when he'd started the chemo. Back then, he was gangling around with his gaunt frame, but now he seemed to have filled out a bit. He looked good. We were spending more and more time together; I accompanied him to his sessions, but we spent a lot of time together outside of that, too. I did live in his house, so it would've been difficult for us to not cross paths every so often, but all this time we were spending together was a familiar feeling, which brought me back to when I was a kid. I used to love spending time with him, following him to the pub. Now, at least, we could share a drink. We could talk.

With Barrie it was still a waiting game. She had to do blood test after blood test, much like Dad had to. I was excited for her arrival, but I had yet to finish the shed where we were supposed to live. It was still uninhabitable, and – in its current condition – was probably a downgrade from our living arrangements in Syria.

I wanted to get it done as soon as I could, but work took over my life in those months. I could hear Netty's words echoing in my ears; she'd said from the beginning that I needed to get on with it. She always knew best.

I knew to expect a smug 'I told you so' in her thick Polish accent if the shed wasn't ready in time for Barrie's arrival.

Sometime in late October, Judith called me with some great news. Any day now Barrie would be allowed to travel. She was so close; I could almost feel her in my arms. Of course, I was entirely unprepared for this, even though I'd been waiting for this moment from the moment I met her, six months prior, almost to the day.

Then, a couple of days later, Judith rang. 'If all goes according to plan, she should be in Heathrow on Saturday.' I couldn't contain my excitement, but she made sure to emphasise *multiple times* that everything needed to go 'according to plan'.

It didn't dampen my excitement, not at all. Barrie had passed the tests, and it didn't matter where I had to go and get her, I was going to get her. I was certain I would be holding her in my arms very soon.

'That's fine, whatever you need me to do. I'll do,' I said to her, confidently. Netty was by my side gripping my arms as the call happened. She shared my excitement and glee.

'I'll call you with any updates.'

And then she hung up. Just like that. My little Barrie was on her way home.

Netty couldn't contain herself. 'Oh my God!' she screamed. 'Oh my God, oh my God, oh my God! It's really happening.'

There was something so casual about it all. I couldn't really comprehend it. Barrie was going to be on a flight from Jordan to London in less than a week. Barrie, the dog I found in Syria, will be in London. In a week. Even thinking about it now, it simply doesn't make any sense. They're just going to fly this dog over, just like that. How is this even happening?

In Heathrow, I'd be waiting for Barrie in the same airport I'd found myself in six months ago, when I first travelled to Syria. Back then, I had not a clue that I was about to embark on the journey of a lifetime, and make a friend for life in the process. I remember wondering about all the people travelling that day, how many different destinations they would reach. I could have never imagined where that one flight (and a few more connecting flights) would bring me. In Heathrow on Saturday, it felt like everything was going to come full circle.

The big event Mitch and I had been planning for months, Warfare, was scheduled for the day after Barrie's arrival. It seemed perfect; I thought I might be able to bring her to it. She might enjoy it – the event consisted of multiple obstacle courses in a massive field. Seemed like the perfect way to introduce Barrie to her new life. She could run around as much as she liked and roll around in the mud. I could picture it all in my head.

'And where is she going to sleep?' Netty asked. I knew this was coming.

'There are still a few things we need to sort out with the shed. The roof needs to be done, and the bed needs to be fitted still. I don't think we'll get it done in time,' I replied.

'I told you so.'

She was so smug, and so Polish. I couldn't help but laugh. It didn't matter where we slept; we could deal with that later. Barrie was coming home, that was all that mattered.

A couple of days later, on Thursday, Judith sends me a text.

It read: 'I don't think she's coming on Saturday. I haven't heard a word from the cargo people, and no one works tomorrow as it's their holy day. I don't think we'll have enough time to figure it out by Saturday, but maybe we could do it on Sunday.'

She did warn me, several times, that everything had to go according to plan. And that I shouldn't get my hopes up too high. But Sunday wasn't too big of a delay, just a day more.

Surely after six months of waiting, another day wasn't too long a wait.

Unfortunately, Sunday was a complicated day for Mitch and me. It was the day of Warfare, and we'd worked tirelessly to make this event happen. It was going to have ten different obstacle courses, four teams. It had a whole storyline to it. It was going to be an incredible event. We were going to really push our clients to their limits. I didn't want to have to divide myself between this and Barrie; I was determined to make Warfare work.

Judith said the flight – 'if all goes according to plan' – would land at 2 p.m., but that Barrie would most likely only be ready to be picked up around 6 p.m., because of all the paperwork they'd need to go through upon arrival.

'That could just about work,' I said to Netty. 'It should be fine.'

'Yeah, just like the shed.'

Did I forget to say Netty was funny? At least she seemed to think she was.

All I had to do was speed off after the event was done, and I could be in Heathrow in less than an hour. *If all goes according to plan*, I snickered to myself.

I awoke on Sunday morning, and couldn't quite believe what I was about to do. Warfare was going to be amazing, but somehow that wouldn't even be the highlight of my day. Everyone was buzzing to meet Barrie, the whole team was feeling giddy about her arrival. I woke up feeling a little queasy about the day I had ahead of me. It was a lot to process. The event was a big deal for us, and Barrie was an even bigger deal.

Mitch and I had piled our equipment in the back of our van the day before, so in the morning we just needed to drive to the Thurrock Rugby Club, where the event was being held, to set up. Simple as. Just around sunrise we set out for what was going to be a momentous day for all of us.

Our van drove around as if it was pregnant, lumbering towards the destination. We couldn't go too quickly, as we had all of our equipment in the van and it was quite heavy. As we drove into the field, the van came to a sudden halt. As much as I pressed on the accelerator, we remained fixed in the same position. I got out of the van to find that our tyres had sunk into the ground. We still had a way to go before we were where we needed to be. Just our luck.

'I can't believe it. Of all things . . .' Mitch looked at me incredulously. I shared the sentiment.

All our equipment was in this van. The event was due to start in less than two hours. I whipped out my phone and called AA recovery.

As I was calling them, Louise started calling me. I told Mitch to call recovery instead, as it was important that I answer this phone call. Louise almost never called me, and when she did, it was always about something pressing.

'Hi Sean,' she said. 'I'm so sorry to have to tell you this, but I don't think Barrie's getting on that flight.'

Apparently, Barrie was incredibly agitated and was going ballistic inside her cage. Because of how aggressively and violently she was behaving, they were unlikely to let her board the flight. She didn't like it in the cage. I'm not sure I could really blame her.

'This is one of the worst cases of anxiety I've ever seen in a dog,' Louise added. Not the news I wanted to hear, especially not when I was dealing with another crisis on the field.

T-90 minutes until our event was meant to start, and I'm looking over at Mitch, who is giving me a look of concern like 'mate, none of our equipment is even set up,' but I was still on the line with Louise, trying to sort out Barrie's travel arrangements.

'Okay, that's not an issue. What are we doing next?' I replied. I just wanted solutions, and Louise was a problem-solver.

'She's not in the airport yet. We've been trying to get her into the van, but it's been a bit of a struggle,' she replied. 'It's going to be a bit of a struggle, but look, we're going to try to get her into the van and maybe she'll be calm by the time we're in the airport.'

It seemed we weren't the only ones having van troubles.

'Thanks, Louise. Keep me posted.'

Mitch, too, had just ended his call with recovery.

'Two hours. That's how long it'll take them to get to us.'

'Fuck.'

Fuck was right. We were utterly fucked. I wasn't sure if we could even get any of our equipment to the site, let alone get it set up in the way we wanted. It was meant to be ten elaborate obstacle courses, with mission objectives, and teams would compete against each other. If we were going to save this event, we were going to have to wing it.

'Should we cancel it?' Mitch asked, with a tone of exasperation. 'Nothing's set up and ready to go. We've got barely an hour to make this work.'

We had to change the event. I couldn't even think about Barrie right now, I had to deal with this, but I worried about her. Worst cases of anxiety *ever*?

Clients were arriving, so I went to speak to them at the meeting point. Some of them had brought warpaint with them, this was how excited they were for this event. I felt even more like I didn't want to disappoint them. We'd been talking about this event like it was going to be an amazing day, and now it was going to turn out like our very first bootcamp. Just a big field with a whole load of nothing in it.

Midway through my brief, Louise called. I took a minute to speak with her.

'She didn't make it onto the flight, Sean. I'll call you back with an update.'

Just like that, my heart sank. But I couldn't mope for too long, because if I didn't concentrate on what was going on, I wouldn't be the only one left disappointed that the day.

By this point I'm just stalling. I radioed my team to see if anyone was ready, but they weren't. The recovery came early, which, considering that everything that could've gone wrong had, was a massive surprise. We had most of our team running 400-metre shuttles with the kit to get it all to the staging area on time. The team were amazing. Mitch and I both agreed. They really put some savage work in that day!

Louise called me back, not even fifteen minutes later. As I said, she was really like the Terminator. Nothing could stop her.

'There are two plans. One could happen, the other is very unlikely to happen.'

'Okay . . .'

'There's a flight on Tuesday to Jordan. You'll spend four days with Barrie there, so you can familiarise yourself with her. Maybe she'll be calmer with you. Then, you'd fly to Heathrow with her on Sunday. Does that work for you?'

'Whatever needs to be done. No drama.'

'There's the more unlikely plan, too.'

'I'm all ears.'

'There are three animals travelling to Paris. You're allowed three animals with one handler, but we'll try to grease some palms and get a fourth put on. I'll give you a call later.'

Just like that I was shifting from one dilemma to the other. One second my head's all about Barrie, the next I've got these clients who expect a gruelling and intense obstacle course, which was sitting in the back of a van. It was an obstacle course in itself to get the equipment to where it needed to be.

Mitch, meanwhile, was talking to the recovery guys. He told them to get the van moving again as soon as they could. At this point there was frenetic panic setting in, and my entire team was confused about what was going on. We had nearly thirty customers who were warming up at the meeting point, none of whom knew that we hadn't set anything up.

Thankfully, a lot of extreme military training doesn't really require much equipment. We had people crawling up the hill, running to checkpoints; there was even a mission where everyone was blindfolded. Which conveniently kept them from seeing us set up, but was also legitimately part of the programme. Somehow, we managed to get most of our equipment set up towards the end, and the event wasn't a total disaster.

Then, Judith rang.

'I'm flying to Paris next week.'

Truthfully, I was so exhausted by this point that I didn't really register what this meant at all.

'Paris?'

'Yes, I'm still talking to Louise, but I might be able to bring Barrie with me.'

'Just let me know where I need to be, and I'll be there.'

This whole day was up and down. I was so confused by the end of it, I didn't know what to believe. I'd thought Barrie was going to be with me on three different occasions, and now I just didn't know.

I was so unsure what the plan was at this point, but Louise said she'd call me later with an update. Warfare ended, and we packed everything and headed to my mate Charlie's place. We all needed to have a drink or two and relax after what had been a chaotic day.

All of the members were knackered but raving about the event. It wasn't until we gave out the medals that we decided to tell them of the hellish set-up we had, and they couldn't believe it!

Charlie had organised a 'Welcome home Barrie' pizza party. He didn't know Barrie didn't make the flight. It was a little depressing, but the pizza was good. At least we had pizza.

You couldn't help but laugh at the situation. Murphy's law was in full effect that day.

'I can't believe our luck, Netty.' I passed her a beer. After the day we'd had, we deserved a nice cold drink.

In the middle of Barrie's welcome party, I got a phone call from Louise. Barrie was going to be on the flight with Judith, and she was going to land in Paris on Saturday. Six days from now.

'You need to be there for the transfer.'

Netty and I booked the Eurotunnel there and then.

17

Warfare left us all mangled and broken. It was exhausting, all of it. Not just the actual bootcamp, but everything leading up to it. Mentally I was completely switched off. The next day I felt sore, and tired. My eyes were droopy, and my body disagreed with just about any position I attempted to lie down in.

The next morning, as I woke up, it hit me that Netty and I had actually bought Eurotunnel tickets. We were going to Paris on Saturday. Paris in France. To pick up my dog.

I started my usual morning workout and I kept thinking about how mad Sunday had been. And then it really hit me – in all the commotion on the day, I hadn't even realised that Louise had set up three different plans to bring Barrie home in less than an hour. She had plane tickets ready for me to go to bloody Jordan in the time it takes most people to make their morning coffee. She was such an impressive woman.

I had five days before Netty and I were headed to Paris, which meant I had five days to get the shed into a liveable condition. It would be nothing fancy, but at least we'd have someplace to sleep. I stripped it of all its contents inside, so that it was just four walls. A friend donated a sofa, which immediately became the centrepiece of our new home. In fact it was the only piece, but it made for a quaint abode.

Friday night Netty came over. We had everything prepared, and by we, I mean Netty prepared everything. She was worried we'd miss the train and insisted that we leave three or four hours early.

'We should leave at 6 a.m., you never know what may happen. There might be traffic. An accident. You don't know.'

'If we leave at eight, we'll have more than enough time to make it.'

We continued to argue for a bit, and I think I made some very valid and convincing points. So, we decided we were going to leave at 6 a.m.

In the morning, we were up bright and early. Netty had barely slept; she essentially acted as the alarm for the alarm. It was still dark out, with just one lamp post outside our front door illuminating a small part of the street. Netty's 2011 Nissan Micra was parked on the pavement just below the lamp post. This was a car that had never been driven more than ten miles; Netty never drove it. I think the furthest she'd ever travelled in this car was when she went to Windsor, west of London, a couple of years back. Roughly a 70-mile journey. Paris Charles de Gaulle was roughly 300 miles away.

'Hey, Netty. You sure this car can make it?' I pressed my foot against the accelerator. It started smoothly, but a few seconds in you could hear a fan belt slipping with an ever-increasing screech until it suddenly calmed. Not a promising sign.

'Yes, it's a car, isn't it?'

In the end I was quite glad we'd chosen to leave earlier. We caught the sunrise, and it meant we could have a more leisurely trip. Enjoy the drive. I loved driving; like back in Syria, it was oddly therapeutic for me. I was freaking out a little bit about Barrie, because we were just five hours away from seeing her. I needed to drive to relax.

Breathe, Sean. Breathe.

I'd spent the entire week wearing the same clothes to bed, without washing them, on the advice of Louise, who said that it would help Barrie recognise my scent. It was a little gross, but these are the things you do for love.

At roughly 7 a.m. we reached Folkestone; we watched the sunrise as we were arriving. We were there roughly two hours before our booking time of 9.30 a.m. It was fine, Netty was right. You can never be too cautious with these things. At the terminal, we were told that we could potentially catch an earlier one, which was a small vindication for Netty. We stopped for breakfast at a LEON near the terminal and I had some muffins and a hot chocolate. I got myself a poppy from someone who was selling them just outside.

'Do you think she'll recognise me?' I asked Netty. It was a combination of small talk and actual concern.

'Maybe not at first, but she will. Of course she will. I think she'll know I'm her mama the moment she sees me, too.'

My concerns continued to grow. Louise had said that Barrie had been extremely aggressive in Jordan, and she was a much larger dog now. Much larger than she was when I used to hold her in my arms. I doubted if I could even still hold her any more.

After breakfast we drove up to the train, but as we approached a red light began to flash. We'd just missed it.

'See, this is why we come early.'

Netty, smug as usual.

We waited in our lane for the light to turn green. Netty was mesmerised by the Eurotunnel, as she'd never been on it before. We drove up a ramp and onto a bridge, and then the train was there waiting for us. The door slid open, and we drove into the train until we reached the end of it.

Netty was freaking out.

'We are in a car, in a train,' she said. 'How crazy is that?'

We're about to go to Paris together, in a 2011 Micra that will probably break down at some point during the trip, to get a dog I found in Syria, so that we could bring her back to Essex where we were going to live in a shed. I'm not sure a car being inside a train really qualified as crazy to me any more.

'Yes, so crazy . . .'

It was a thirty-odd minute journey to Calais. We knew we were in France when we got off because, well, the signs were all in French. We stopped by a petrol station as soon as we arrived. Netty was tasked with paying. It was 2018 after all. But Netty couldn't figure out how to pay. She kept looking around like a lost puppy while flailing her card around hoping someone would notice her.

Suddenly there was a voice over the tannoy in French; I think she was trying to indicate to Netty where the payment area was. I tried pointing towards the area myself, but Netty just gave me a quizzical look as if pointing was no longer a universally understood concept.

'Over there!' I muttered, while still pointing at the payment kiosk. I opened my eyes wider, as if to tell her to look where I was looking. It couldn't have been more obvious.

The builders decided to call me now, while we were at the critical point, to tell me they were not happy to do the roof of the shed. Netty was so close to being able to pay, but now she had to do it without my guidance.

I couldn't even be bothered with the builders at this point, I just wanted to get Barrie back. If we had a leaky roof, we had a leaky roof. Barrie has lived through worse, so have I.

By divine intervention, surely, Netty managed to find the payment kiosk and paid for our petrol. Our road trip to Charles de Gaulle could finally resume.

I enjoyed winding Netty up. Her reactions just always gave me a spark of joy. She was so easily annoyed, and she'd always roll her eyes at me. A bit like how Barrie did. I had a whole country playlist with me. Netty absolutely hated country music. I kept it on for most of the trip, but she didn't say anything. I think she didn't want to give me the satisfaction. Johnny Cash. Willie Nelson. Brad Paisley. Only the best of country for Netty. We kept it on until Netty finally had enough. Then I had to endure the songs from the musical *Greatest Showman*, which itself is very good and a good film, but Netty sings it loud and proud!

'Okay, come on, Sean. Change it.'

With about an hour to go, she caved. Worth it.

It took about two and a half hours to get to the airport. Nothing really happened on our way there. Netty and I spoke about Barrie a lot. She tried to ignore the country music that was blaring from the speakers. The closer we got to the airport, the more I felt I was going to shit myself.

We parked and headed to Arrivals.

While we waited, what we were doing started to make less and less sense to me. I was just standing here at Arrivals like everyone else, waiting to be reunited with their loved ones. I imagined it might be like in those Hollywood films, where I would spot Barrie at one end of the room while I was at the other. Our eyes would meet, and we would start running towards each other.

I don't know why I thought this would be possible. I mean, firstly, she's a dog. If our eyes were going to meet, I'd have to be on all fours. Secondly, she would probably be in a cage, so if my eyes were going to meet anyone else's, it would probably be Judith's. Thirdly, did I mention she's a dog?

I was so nervous. I looked up at the arrivals board. I looked for the Jordan flight. It had landed early, so Barrie should be out soon.

I was shaking, holding this dirty top I'd worn to bed all week, feeling incredibly silly.

'Calm down, Sean.'

'I am calm. You calm down.'

I sure showed her.

People were beginning to stare at me. I think maybe they thought I was one of those tear-jerking stories you always see of military folk meeting their family members after a prolonged time at war, as I had my military bag and military dog harness with me.

We waited for about forty-five minutes. I shuffled about nervously, pacing around in tiny circles. We saw countless people come and go, but not Barrie. Where was she?

Maybe this was all too good to be true. In my life, this entire story was just so out of place. Barrie and I reuniting? That would have been out of character. It wouldn't have fitted with the comedy that was my life. Getting stood up by a dog? That was more my pace. Or the flight suddenly being cancelled or rerouted, that would have made more sense.

I started panicking a little. *A little a lot.*

'I can hear dogs!' I bellowed.

I don't know how many dogs there were, but they all sounded incredibly violent and certainly unfriendly. Judith came through the doors shortly after that. From the barking I thought there might have been at least four massive dogs, a suspicion only heightened by the fact that she came out with three or four crates. But when she got to us, there were no other dogs. That fury wasn't that of four angry mutts, it was of one. Barrie. *My* Barrie.

She was losing her mind. She wasn't the cute little pupper I'd found in Syria; she was this aggressive big dog. Like my neighbour's who bit me when I was a kid. I started shaking, but very gently, trying my best to hide it from everyone.

I laughed at the thought of the neighbour's dog. It reminded me of when I first met Barrie. I'd been scared she might bite me when she was just the size of a football, and I felt the same way now. She was scared, too, not aggressive. Just as she was when I found her for the first time. I couldn't even imagine how scary this entire experience was for her. I knew I'd have to regain her trust, just as I had in Syria.

I remembered her, even if she looked so wildly different. I hoped she remembered me. I don't think I'd changed much in appearance, so really she had no excuses.

I had this old T-shirt I'd been wearing for a week with me and, as silly as it seemed, I gave it a go.

'This is so silly, Netty.' I laughed. Nervously.

'Just do it. Come on.'

No faffing about with Netty. I was just having a mental breakdown.

I extended my arm out gently towards Barrie's cage, holding the T-shirt firmly in my fist. The closer I got to her, the sillier this felt. And, to the shock of absolutely no one, it didn't work. She just looked at me like I was crazy before unleashing an onslaught of barks, each one mightier than the last.

'Come on, we need to get her to your car.' Judith interrupted this moment of utter madness.

'I don't think she recognises me,' I whispered to Netty. I was genuinely saddened by this; for all the pessimism I'd shown throughout the day, I had actually been hopeful she'd remember me. 'She has no clue who I am.'

We weren't reunited in the way I'd imagined in my head. Not that silly Hollywood running across the airport nonsense. Instead, we were just an angry dog and a scared soldier at an airport. Seven months had led to this moment, and now I just felt sad. If she didn't recognise me now, would she ever?

'Don't worry about it too much,' Judith said, reassuringly. 'It'll always take some time. She's had a long, long journey here.'

Yeah. Long was true.

From Syria, to Iraq, to Jordan, to Paris. Now she was about to set off on a car ride to Essex with someone she didn't even recognise.

She was seething and growling as we wheeled her towards the car park. It was still light out, and we thought it might be good for her to have a little run around. Get those legs working a bit. So we stopped on the way. We opened the cage, Judith struggled to put the lead on her and I – rather ambitiously – tried to pet her, but she was having none of it.

I tried to walk her around to have a wee, I knew she loved doing that, but she was so scared that her legs were trembling and she wouldn't lower herself. It was clear that this was going to be a long process.

We put her back into her cage and took her to the basement parking where our mighty Micra waited for us. We tried to walk her around the car park as well. We did a few slow rounds, slowly strolling by all the parked cars.

'Just don't bite me, all right, Barrie,' I asked, in a hushed tone. 'It's me. Sean.'

She just looked up at me like 'who's this geezer?' I stroked her head a little bit, and Judith decided this was the point when she had to go.

'All the best, Sean. Pleasure to meet the two of you. Well, three of you.'

She approached Barrie and told her she'd miss her too. Netty was on the verge of tears. Judith, just like everyone who was a part of Barrie's story, had got so attached to this dog. It felt strange to say she was my dog – it felt like she was everyone's dog. Although, right now, I was trying to establish if she was anyone's dog.

There was an additional surprise. For some reason we'd thought we were going to put Barrie in the backseat of the Micra. We didn't know we had to bring with us the crate she'd come with. It was massive, and it absolutely didn't fit in the back of this tiny Nissan.

We had to pry the crate open, splitting it in half, and stacked one half over the other so that it could fit in the back. The way Barrie sat inside the half of the crate reminded me of the way she'd sat in the fruit basket back in Syria. It was the spitting image of the way she was then. It was the same type of thing as well, two boxes stacked on top of each other. I felt this bout of nostalgia overcome me. This is my Barrie – she doesn't know it now, but it's her.

The Micra was quite cramped. It wasn't made for two passengers and a massive dog. Barrie had her head sticking through the middle of the two front seats. I just hoped she wouldn't bite me while I was driving.

'Barrie, if you're even considering biting me, I just want you to consider road safety. It's not just my life at risk, it's the other motorists we need to think about.'

She didn't bite me. Instead she fell asleep almost as soon as we started driving back. Her bark might have changed, but her snore was exactly the way I remembered it. We drove for about an hour to the chorus of her snores. I think Netty would have preferred the country music to this.

We stopped in Lens at around 4 p.m., for a quick toilet break. Barrie woke up and Netty and I agreed this could be another chance to get her outside for a bit, before it got dark.

Barrie was quite calm at this point, but we didn't really know what to expect when we opened the boot of the car. We didn't know if we were about to unleash Barrie or if we were opening the gates for a lion to escape. Just in case, we'd brought with us many treats to bribe her with. They were the fancy kind, the kind we probably wouldn't be able to afford ever again but that we'd anticipated we might need today.

Barrie got out. It was a little chilly out and I hoped she wasn't feeling too cold. She didn't bark, she didn't pounce on me. She was calm. I walked around in circles in the car park, just slowly guiding her around. To make her feel comfortable. She followed my leg closely as I moved around, and then she started sniffing my thigh.

It was a quiet and intimate moment. We continued to walk around in circles. I was prepared to do this until she wanted to stop. Then, she started circling me like a shark. She was curious. Maybe I reminded her of something. She sniffed me once more, trying to get a better whiff of me. I considered taking out the old T-shirt but then thought better of it.

'I think she's recognising me, Netty.'

'I think she is, too.'

After a moment of deliberation, I think something clicked. Barrie fell to the ground by my feet, her belly facing up and her paws reaching out for me. She wanted to play. She knew who I was.

'Who's a good girl?' I asked. I'd waited so long to ask her that.

18

We played for a few moments longer in that parking lot in Lens. It felt like a dream; I was pinching myself constantly. I couldn't believe I was really there with Barrie. In some ways I didn't want this to end, as though leaving would hex it and we'd be lost again to each other for ever.

But it was now nearing 9 p.m., the weak sun had long since given up the ghost and the November air was decidedly chilly. It was time to set off to Calais. This was the next test. How would she take to the car? I had no idea. She was a big dog. If something spooked her and she started kicking off in the back, God knows what would happen. Nervously we put the backseats down and eased Barrie into the crate.

'There's a good girl,' I said, soothingly. I listened for the little groan she used to emit in Syria whenever she had to move – the grumble as if to say, 'Oh, life's too hard.' I couldn't detect anything. This was my Barrie, right? I patted her gently and waited to see if there was a reaction.

To our relief she settled down nicely. Perhaps the exertions of the last twenty-four hours were catching up with her. As we set off, gingerly at first, she sat in her crate but poked her head out and nestled it between the window and the front passenger seat where Netty was sitting, resting her head on her shoulder. Netty started stroking her head. Barrie seemed to like that. Her eyes closed. This was more like it. Peaceful, she looked more like her old self, the way she did when we rode together back in Syria. I began to reminisce about all those car rides we took together, in and out of Raqqa. It seemed surreal, so distant. Not even a year had passed since Barrie and I were in that war zone, our realities a far cry from what they were going to be now. It was all so vivid though. I remembered it all – Barrie, perched on our vehicle's window, watching the world go by. I used to imagine what it would be like if she could look out those dusty Land Cruisers and see fields, and flowers, and cows – not dust, rubble and lifelessness. I didn't have to imagine any more; Barrie was in my car, this tiny never-used Nissan Micra, and outside was a whole hopeful world waiting for her.

I thought about everything I wanted to show her – my house, my friends, my hometown. I wanted to bring her to work, show her off to everyone. Suddenly, it all felt real.

It's odd. You spend so long imagining what a single event will feel like, how it will change your life, and when it actually happens, you just feel speechless. Paralysed at the sheer incredulity of the moment. Thankfully, I was still able to drive despite the metaphorical paralysis, but I really couldn't believe it.

I was taking nothing for granted though. Although it was only an hour's drive to Calais, it was a long, nervous journey. Barrie was seemingly quite content to have Netty stroking her head with her eyes closed but I worried that at any moment she might wake up and, unsure of her surroundings, freak out.

I needn't have worried. She pretty much slept the whole way to Calais. Before we headed for the train we had a bit of time to kill, so we stopped off at McDonald's to get some food. Barrie was still zonked out, only stirring to have a sniff, scratch and stretch. We counted our blessings and carried on to the train.

'We have all the documents, right?' Netty asked, once the train began moving.

I could tell she was nervous because that was about the hundredth time she'd asked me! I reassured her that we had everything we needed; we'd prepared for this. *She'd* prepared for this.

'What if they don't let Barrie and me in? You know, Brexit is coming,' she said, trying to humour me, knowing I was nervous.

'You've nothing to worry about, you're a British citizen,' I said. 'As for Barrie, she has managed to get through the border in Syria, Iraq, and Jordan,' I said. 'She's not getting stopped in bloody Blighty!'

For all my bold words though, I was just as anxious as she was. This was the next big test. We arrived on the UK side and had to drive to a special pet entrance. This was something I'd obviously never had to do before, so I wasn't entirely sure what was due to happen. I got Barrie out of the car. She seemed to sense my nervousness as she tucked herself into my side for the short walk over to the officer. This was the moment of truth. It was 10.45 p.m. and I wasn't sure if the lateness of the hour might work in our favour should there be an issue. It would be a long way back to France if there were a problem. I don't know how long the officer had been on shift but his demeanour said he'd rather be somewhere else.

'Paperwork,' he said. I handed it over.

He brought out a little scanner and moved it over Barrie's body. She stood good as gold but I had a momentary flutter, suddenly getting a wave of fear – what if her details didn't match the documentation? Would we have to go back to France and be stuck there until it was cleared up? There was a pause that seemed to last half a lifetime, then:

'Perfect,' he said. 'You're good to go.'

Fantastic! The documents were in order. War Paws had come up trumps.

Barrie was as good as home!

The next stage of our journey seemed to fly by. It was an hour and a half from Folkestone to home, so we stopped at Ashford to let Barrie stretch her legs and do her business.

At Lens she'd lain down to wee, something the War Paws people said she would do until she felt more comfortable. When she climbed out of the car at Ashford she was still a bit guarded. She had a sniff of the air but stuck quite close to my leg – and to Netty's. She didn't want to wander too far. But then it was as though she could tell she was almost at her final destination. I watched as she squatted and weed, just like any normal female dog does. It sounds such an inconsequential thing but it was like we had reached another landmark. By that simple gesture, it was clear she felt more relaxed, and by the way she hung close to my leg I was convinced the old bond with me was crystallising in her head. All we had to do now was get her home.

It was 12.30 a.m. by the time we pulled up at my parents' home. The same single lamp post lit the front of their house and I parked the Micra right under it. Perhaps the most incredible part of this entire story was that, against all odds, this Micra had made it there and back without a hitch.

I woke Barrie up, and attached her lead to her collar. We walked out; this was her new home. I let her sniff around, gather her senses a bit. As crazy as this was for me, it must have been absolutely mental for her.

'C'mon, Barrie. Let's go in, this is our new home,' I said, as I took her in the side gate. I didn't want to walk her in through the house just yet because of Dad's allergy. She went into the garden first of all and had a nose about. Then she went up to the shed and had a sniff about there. My mum and dad were standing in the kitchen where glass doors look onto the garden. Mum doesn't really like big dogs and at the sight of Barrie wandering around the garden, I could see her mouth, 'Oh my God, she's huge!'

Looking at Barrie in our garden, I could see Mum was right. She was huge. She used to have such short pudgy legs; even when she tried to run, she never covered much ground, but her legs were long now. She looked fast and, despite her epic travels, appeared in good nick, beautiful in fact.

'Wow,' I said to Netty. 'Barrie's home.' I could scarcely believe we'd made it.

We led her towards the shed and she took a tentative sniff inside. It didn't take her long to start exploring inside.

'Look, Barrie, your new bed,' I said, patting the one I'd got for her. She looked at me as if to say, 'Yes, very good,' and jumped up on the bed. After a quick sniff she circled a couple of times, had a scratch of the bedclothes with her paw, and slumped bang in the middle of it.

That was my Barrie! Just like she'd done in Syria.

She got comfy – and there it was. The little groan I knew so well, and had missed so much.

'Life is hard,' Barrie was saying.

Maybe, my friend. But now it was going to get a whole lot better – for all of us.

19

'Woof! Woof!'

Was I dreaming? We'd all crashed out so completely the night before – exhausted from the endless travelling and mental rollercoaster – that it took me a few moments to work out what was happening when I first came to.

It was 8 a.m. and we were in the shed. And it was Barrie barking to be let out into the garden!

I was amazed at how quickly it felt like having the old Barrie back. Jumping into the middle of the bed, chewing any piece of wood she could find – it was like we were back in Syria. She was doing all the same things she had done in my room out there. I let her out to do her essentials and then she bounded back in, up onto my chest, looking to play, her tail wagging uncontrollably from left to right. It immediately put a smile on my face, although I was struggling to breathe, as I still wasn't used to how heavy she'd become. I don't think she quite realised how big she was either.

'Morning to you too, Barrie. You do know you're not a tiny little pup any more, right?' I said, as she weighed me down, sinking me deep into the mattress. One thing was clear. Barrie was up. We all had to get up. She had her big new world to explore. First things first – we had to take her up to the house. She was a bit unsure of what lay beyond the glass doors into the kitchen. She put her front feet in first and had a big sniff, trying to detect any familiar scents. Then she edged herself in and had a look around. My parents' kitchen is L-shaped and the first thing she encountered was the dining table, with the fridge-freezer next to that. She had a good nose around but that was all she was getting to see. She had a track record for weeing in all the most inappropriate places, and leaving a liquid present for Mum and Dad wouldn't be the way to ingratiate herself! If she behaved, then over time she might get to explore the rest of the house.

At first my mum was a bit scared of her but once she let Barrie have a good sniff of her a bond was formed. Before long it was like Mum had another grandchild! She's among the worst for sneaking Barrie treats. As for my dad, he was fine with her. He started to suffer a bit of a reaction the longer he spent with her but she's not aggravated his allergy as much as we feared.

'I can't believe she's here. She's actually here. She's actually real,' Dad said. I couldn't believe it either. He had a proud look on his face; of everything I'd done in my life, I think this was the one thing that made him the proudest.

It put a smile on my face. Dad was always the biggest influence in my life. I wanted to be just like him. Any situation he was put in, he always came away smelling like a rose.

We lived in a horrible place growing up, and now we lived in this beautiful home. The house Barrie and I now lived in, that was something he'd built from nothing.

Sitting there, sharing a tea with Dad, I felt like I'd made him proud. I was becoming more like him. We never wanted anything as kids, but Dad always made sure to provide for us. There were years where he was out of a job, but he was always out working. Three or four jobs, but you'd never know. I'd get back from school, and he'd always find the time for us. I was shit in school, but every night he'd help me drill my maths homework. 'Discipline, discipline, discipline,' he used to say. He always took time to work on it. He had that mindset. Problems were nothing to worry about. They were only things waiting for solutions. Even with the cancer, he was never down; never let himself get overcome with emotion. He just looked for solutions. He might never have been in a war like I had, but he was still a fighter.

'No drama, Dad,' I said. That's what my dad would do, when something went wrong; there was never any drama.

I wanted to be for Barrie what Dad was for me.

Once the initial introductions were over we let Barrie have a little wander around to familiarise herself with the sights and sounds of the garden. It's not the biggest space in the world but for Barrie it might as well have been another planet. There must have been a thousand different sounds and smells she had to get used to. The charity had said not to take her out on any long walks for the first few days we had her at home. The priority was getting her to the vets to be checked over, so an appointment was made for a few days' time. Then it was important to get her acclimatised to home for three or four days. If we introduced her to too many things too early there was a danger she'd cave in. So on that first day I played with her in the garden and tried to work out how much of her training she'd remembered from Syria. The short answer? Not a thing!

In Syria Barrie had pretty much always been off the lead. Knowing we were going to have many unforced months apart, my plan there had been to train her really well so she'd know a host of commands and tricks that would be locked in for when she came home. I'd been amazed at how quickly she'd picked up commands. She was a permanent fixture by my side in the camp. We had a makeshift lead for her when I was out on tasks, purely for her own safety, but otherwise she didn't need it. I quickly realised that she had completely forgotten all I'd taught her! The hours I'd spent training her as a puppy had meant nothing.

One encouraging factor, though, was how healthy her appetite was. I'd given her meals in the shed and she had so far scoffed them down like no tomorrow. That was a relief. Another concern was how she'd adapt to dog food here. In the camp in Syria there had been working dogs, so I'd had access to dry kibble, but not a lot. For the most part I'd given Barrie some of the kibble, whatever meat we had been having, and some rice. The chefs there had been really good; even if there hadn't been rice on the menu they'd cook me up some for Barrie. That wasn't a bad diet for a stray dog and, although she would have been eating normal dog food during her stay in the kennels, I wondered whether she'd associated me with the good life and now we were reunited would she expect more of the same? Thankfully, that didn't seem to be the case. So far so good.

I'd taken the next week off work; the only thing I was going to do was help out with a bootcamp on Wednesday. I was looking forward to concentrating on spending time with Barrie – just a nice, relaxing time to ease her gently into her new life.

If only!

When I'd first rescued her I'd had a few people contact me asking to represent her, so I had an inkling the story could be quite big. So right from the start I documented everything we did. When I went to collect Barrie with Netty we'd taken loads of pictures, so on the Saturday we took some time to update my social media. 'We've got Barrie! Look at her!' That sort of stuff.

Another person to contact me while I was still out in Syria was a journalist, Joe Pagnelli. Joe worked for an agency in Birmingham. 'I think your story's got legs,' he said. 'I really like it and I'd like to write the story.'

I hadn't thought too much about it at that stage. 'Okay,' I said. 'Sweet.'

Once I'd come back to England, I gave him a call to keep him updated. Now we had her safely back home I gave him another shout. We wanted to put the story out about Barrie's epic journey and how we were reunited. We chatted over the phone and he wrote up the story.

Three days' peace and quiet was all we had before suddenly we were all over the national press!

The first I knew was when it started to appear in the online editions of the papers. Friends were sending me links to all these articles.

'Sean, your face is on the *Daily Mail*!'

My phone started ringing and buzzing every other second with calls, texts, messages, emails and social media notifications.

'*British soldier reunited with dog*' said one headline. It was nuts. This thing had just happened to me, it was my reality, and it was now on the internet for everyone to see. It almost seemed like people knew more about it than I did. My life was out there for everyone to read.

The Times, the *Guardian*, the *Sun*, all the big national papers, had the story and it was getting read on the newspaper reviews on live TV on the news channels. Suddenly, foreign websites were picking up the story – Germany, Italy, France, even Colombia!

Our social media then hit the roof. People were sharing and linking photos and videos from my posts. Some of them were creating their own montage videos. I couldn't go online without seeing a video of Barrie and me. It was crazy. Before too long my phone couldn't cope. It was dying within three hours from constantly ringing, pinging with notifications from Facebook, Twitter and Instagram. Most of the time it was people saying, 'Well done for what you've achieved.' I heard from friends and family I hadn't spoken to for years.

People were telling me I was in this newspaper and that. I have friends in Australia and they sent pictures of their newspapers that we were in. People in China who I had never met sent me photos of Barrie. My phone just didn't stop.

It was all very strange. The only time we soldiers are ever mentioned in the papers is when it's an obituary. This was a wholesome story, a welcome change, I thought. There was always a separation in my life between who I was as a civilian and who I was as a soldier; people back home never knew Sean the soldier – but this story bridged that gap. Old friends were telling me how amazing the story was. People were sharing it with their friends and family. Everyone seemed to be saying how uplifting it was.

I'd lived a lot of my life in doubt, not only in my own abilities, but also of who I was as a person. I wondered if I was a good person, someone who was respected. Throughout my teenage years I struggled with that feeling of worthlessness, and after Afghanistan – and all the shitty things I did, all the selfish things I did – I wondered if that was just who I was. Barrie's story brought us to everyone's newsfeeds, and suddenly people saw me as more than just a fuck-up who dropped out of school.

In the next couple of hours I had to accept it – Barrie and I had gone viral!

We had a couple of options – sit back and watch the whole show unfold, or try to regain a bit of control.

'We need to get Barrie her own Instagram account!' Netty said, as always thinking two steps ahead.

'Really?'

'Yeah, it'll be really cute. There's obviously a demand. We'll put little captions as if she is the one talking.'

'Whatever you think,' I laughed. If she wanted to do it, she could go for it.

Over the next forty-eight hours, our story continued to make the rounds. Barrie and I were in actual printed newspapers; I don't think I'd ever purchased a newspaper before in my life, but I did that day. Our story was out there, in black and white, sent to doorsteps, offices and coffee shops across the UK.

That wasn't all. I got a call from a woman from *This Morning* – the ITV show!

'Eamonn and Ruth want to do the story,' she said.

Eamonn and Ruth? As in Eamonn Holmes and his wife Ruth Langsford?! They wanted to speak to me on live TV about a dog? The world had gone mad! Wow, this was huge.

To do it we'd have to go to London on Friday. They would send a car to pick us up and take us all the way there. It sounded too good to turn down.

I was getting more requests too, from Lorraine Kelly's show, BBC Radio 2, among others. Among the stranger approaches was one from a company called The Dodo. They explained they were one of the biggest social media companies for dogs in the world. Who knew there was such a thing? They could help us take Barrie's profile to a whole new level.

Next it was a call from Fiona, an editor at the publishers Hodder and Stoughton. She said how much she loved our story, thought it would make a brilliant book, and could she meet me. It was mind-boggling. Joe's agency now came in handy because I had been fielding loads of media requests; now I put everyone on to the agency so they could deal with all the phone calls. I'd had so many I didn't know what to do. I'd never experienced anything like this.

This Morning had called first and they wanted us to be exclusive, meaning we couldn't appear anywhere else first. As great as the other requests were, I felt we had to go with them. I couldn't really think of anyone better to do the story with. It was all arranged for Friday. I also made plans to meet Fiona at Hodder while we were there to discuss their ideas for a book. It was all happening.

'Well, Barrie,' I said. 'Are you ready for your close-up? You're going to be famous!'

She cocked her head, like she did when she didn't have a clue what I was on about. That about summed it up!

Now we'd committed to *This Morning* we didn't book anything else in. Perhaps now things would die down, we thought. Not a bit of it!

The reaction was still out of this world. I watched as, following the coverage in the national media, my Instagram followers soared by about 7,000 people.

'I never expected any of this,' I said to Netty while lying on the bed, staring up at the ceiling. Netty was a permanent fixture now with Barrie and me. 'It's so crazy.'

'What you mean is this is great,' she said, smiling. 'After

everything you've been through, you deserve this. So does Barrie.'

'I don't know, I don't know if I do deserve any of thi—'

'Shut up, Sean,' she said, before slapping my head.

Rude, I thought.

'In the papers, they're saying I'm all these things. But they don't know me.' I was whispering, as Barrie was still asleep beside me. 'People are talking to me, but they don't even know who I am. It feels like bullshit.'

'I know you. I know you're a good person. You've given this beautiful dog a new life.'

She pointed at Barrie with a sympathetic smile. She was in a deep sleep, oblivious to the fuss being made about her.

She was right, as she always seemed to be. I needed Netty in my life as much as I needed Barrie. She was my rock; she gave me solidity. This was a turbulent time in my life. It seems silly when compared to a war zone, but this was completely new territory for me. And I was beginning to feel claustrophobic with all the attention.

It's funny, in my life everything seemed to happen to me all at once. The only instance when I've ever been afforded time to process anything in my own time was in therapy, where I could go through the emotions at my own pace. For the most part, though, it would all hit at once. Like a freight train with no brakes. I barely knew how to react.

In less than a week, I was centre stage for the first time in my life. People, complete strangers, were messaging me after reading about us. They told me I was a good man; animal lovers showered me with love and gratitude.

'What you did for that dog is incredible!'

'You're so brave for what you did!'

'On behalf of all animal lovers, thank you!'

It was strange. I'd never felt valued in my life. I never felt like I had any worth, and suddenly everyone was telling me I was this great guy. I had people message me, thanking me for my service; some people called me a war hero. As the attention grew, so too did the old feelings that I was an impostor. *How could this all be true?* I asked myself. I knew who I was. I was never a war hero; I was never a great guy. I never even loved animals as a kid; I was scared shitless of dogs.

As I have said, I have always struggled with my sense of identity, of purpose, of worth. I lacked all of it. Suddenly I was being labelled in ways that were the opposite to how I saw myself.

I thought about some of the decisions I'd made in the past. How selfish I was, how reckless and senseless my actions were. How I treated others and disregarded the people who loved me. I thought about Nic. I wasn't a great guy; how could I be?

I've always closed myself from the world. Everything I was feeling, I used to shove into that box. Allowing to pile on, and on, and on. It was the only way to cope; even though I'd learned to ditch that box, I was still learning how to access my emotions, and how to process them, but I was still afraid of everything that was floating in that head of mine. Things I've yet to understand. I was a timorous kid – well, adult now – and yet in a few days I would be speaking about my life in public.

Just as I was drifting into more maudlin thoughts, however, Barrie stood up, gave herself a shake and looked at me, as if to say, 'Come on. What's happening?'

I laughed. 'I'll take my lead from you, Barrie. If you're okay with all this, so am I!'

Friday's television appearance was still a few days away. Before all of that was the bootcamp we had organised. I was going to take Barrie along as part of her acclimatisation process.

I suspected this was going to be a big challenge for her – but I didn't appreciate how big. Since we'd arrived home she'd pretty much been in the garden. This was going to be her first time out and the first time she'd met so many people in one place since we'd been reunited. I had no idea how she'd react.

Netty came with me and we got to the big field where the bootcamp was going to take place. Barrie got out of the car and we let her wander about. She looked completely freaked out. It took us a moment to work out why. Barrie had never been in a big field of grass before! It was completely new to her. Back in Syria you were lucky if you saw a blade of the green stuff. It was a dustbowl. Not only that but when people started to come up to her she started to freak out. She was very wary of people, and of men in particular. That was strange. I wasn't expecting it because back in Syria she was around men all the time and had always seemed relaxed in their company. She definitely wasn't relaxed now. Seeing such a crowd – and with everyone wanting to come up and stroke her and make a fuss – took her by surprise. Everyone was like, 'Oh my God, it's Barrie,' and bounding over, right in her face. She went nuts and crouched down, growling or barking with her teeth bared. She wasn't being aggressive; it was more defensive, like she was just trying to protect herself. She didn't approach the person, she was clearly just saying 'Don't come any closer' and then hiding behind Netty or me, going backwards as she was doing it.

That said, everyone was so respectful towards her, knowing her ordeal. Once they'd said their hellos they got on with the session and ignored her, which was good and bad. Barrie loves attention, even though she was growling to be left alone. As soon as everyone went off and started the boot-camp she wanted to be friends, now she realised she wasn't the centre of attention. She had a long way to go but this was a good start.

When it was over and we got her home she was perfectly fine. She ate her food and settled down. But as I patted her that night I realised we were at the foot of our biggest learning curve yet. It was going to be huge. I just hadn't realised how much she still needed to learn.

20

This was the life! The five-star treatment. This must be what it was like for celebrities all the time. Being picked up and driven everywhere. Maybe I could get used to this!

It was Friday morning, one week after we'd picked Barrie up in France, and we were on our way to the ITV studios in London for our first ever live television appearance.

The team at *This Morning* sent an Addison Lee car for Netty, Barrie and me and on our way we chatted excitedly about what it might be like and what famous people we might see. We were like a couple of kids on our way to Walt Disney World. Barrie seemed pretty chilled, like she did this all the time. I wasn't taking anything for granted, however. I knew this was going to be a big ask for her and I just hoped she didn't get too freaked out.

For most of the way she slept. That was until we entered central London and all the noises and general hustle and bustle peaked her interest. It dawned on us then that Barrie hadn't actually been in such a large density of people before. She was instantly curious but guarded. And we found out very quickly that she doesn't like moped or scooter riders!

As we passed through the busy streets she growled at any passing moped.

I thought I'd considered every eventuality but I should have known by now that, with Barrie, it's the things you never think of that catch you out. Our driver arrived at the studios and we walked in. Everything was fine – until, that is, someone explained to us that the *This Morning* studio was on the first floor. Okay, no problem. We headed to the stairs. Wait a moment. Barrie got to the bottom step, looked up, and sat down. I gave her a tug on the lead. 'Come on, Barrie, up we go.'

She pulled back with her head. Her front paws were spread and she backed up on her bottom.

Netty laughed. Then I got it.

'Oh shit! She doesn't know what stairs are!' I said. 'She's never seen them before.'

Everything in our house was on the one level. In her short life she'd never had to climb stairs. I pulled again.

'Come on, Barrie, it's fine. They're just stairs.'

Netty moved one or two up to show there was no drama, but Barrie wasn't having any of it. And, as I was discovering, when she sets her mind to something it's hard to persuade her otherwise.

There was no alternative. I had to carry her. I hoisted her up. What a difference a few months makes! Barrie was now twenty-seven kilos of heavy, and when you're lifting that up a flight of steps you feel it!

'Bloody hell!' I said to Netty when I'd got her to the top

of the stairs. 'If this is what stairs do to her, what's she going to be like with all the lights and the people in there?'

Netty smiled and shrugged. 'We'll take it as it comes.'

Good answer.

Any concerns I had were quickly dispelled by the *This Morning* team. They couldn't have been nicer or friendlier. They were very cool. They showed us into our own private room for Barrie to sit in and gave her some water. That was perfect. It allowed us to take a breath and get our bearings.

Then it began. Loads of people started coming to the door. Word had clearly got out that Barrie was in the building. They were all so sweet, going, 'Oh wow, it's Barrie!'

Bearing in mind how she'd been at the bootcamp, though, I got a bit protective.

'That's great,' I said, 'but she doesn't like being crowded. Would you mind coming in one at a time to say hello? She's really defensive and not really a people person at the moment.'

To be fair, everyone did as I asked and in a matter of seconds there were six or seven people, some of them famous faces I recognised off the TV, queuing outside our room to catch a glimpse of our dog! I stood there like a bouncer on crowd control for the big star. It was the Friday before Remembrance Sunday and a lot of the news programmes were reporting on soldiers and mental health, so our story fitted in there quite well. There were a couple of former soldiers around and they came up to introduce themselves.

They were two Welsh lads, Dorian and Matt, who were veterans from tours of Iraq. They'd both come back with serious PTSD. They were giving an interview about the condition's ramifications for their daily lives, something I could relate to. We spoke a bit about the effects of the war, how they became depressed and despondent, and how they were making choices they never would've made before. They showed me some videos on their phones that they took before they went to Iraq. They were positive, confident, funny. They were all those things until they weren't. They were afraid, too, that any progress they made would suddenly be undone. I'd thought I was the only one.

'You've just got to stay on top of it,' Dorian said. 'Just got to stay on top of it, always.'

I nodded. That was certainly true. I thanked them for coming over and we shook hands and parted, wishing each other well.

All the while Barrie was taking it in her stride but I was still a bit apprehensive about the actual studio in which we'd be filming. I said to one of the producers: 'I know this will be going out live, but is there any chance I could take her up to the studio a little bit early to get her used to the surroundings?'

'No problem,' she said.

What they did next was really cool. The crew had planned a pre-recorded section for later in the programme but they said they would move it around in the schedule to go out before our slot so we wouldn't disturb the broadcast. That meant I could take Barrie to the studio and get her settled while viewers at home watched the pre-recorded item. When I took Barrie to the studio there was Eamonn and Ruth. Again, I didn't really know what to expect. I hadn't really been around any famous people, except for when I was in the military and the odd celebrity came to visit us. Whatever thoughts I'd had, Eamonn and Ruth were not what I expected. They were so nice and normal. Ruth came over and gave me a massive hug and was all over Barrie, asking me loads of cute questions about her. Eamonn said the combination of me being a soldier and the dog I'd rescued from the rubble must have been doing wonders for my love life!

'No,' I said, 'that's my missus over there!'

Netty gave me a quizzical look, as if to say, 'What? Am I?'

Believe it or not, despite the amount of time we spent together this still wasn't something we'd discussed – what our status was. Were we boyfriend and girlfriend? It certainly felt like the most natural thing in the world being with her and she'd practically never left my side in weeks. Plus, we'd been through so much together with Barrie. Neither of us had asked the question though. And now was not the time to have that discussion. We were about to go live on air!

We sat on a plush blue sofa in the back room of the studio, waiting to come on. Barrie seemed completely calm and unfazed by any of the bright lights and commotion that lit up the studio. As the seconds counted down I, on the other hand, was properly bricking it. I was so nervous; I didn't want to say the wrong thing – actually, I wasn't sure I wanted to say anything at all.

'How are you so calm, Barrie?' I asked. She looked at me with a blank stare and then tilted her head up, nudging me to scratch her neck.

In the end it was done and dusted in a flash. Eamonn and Ruth couldn't have been nicer. Their questions were gentle and I just spoke honestly. It felt very natural and, thanks to them, once the cameras started rolling I was completely at ease.

Barrie was a natural in front of the camera. From the moment she went into the studio she lay down and did her own thing, pretty oblivious to what was going on. We did the interview and when we came off screen we went backstage again to get our stuff. Then it was time to get in our car to head to our next appointment with Hodder and Stoughton.

On the way my phone rang. It was someone from Sky News.

'Hi, we've just seen you on *This Morning*. Can you come and be live on the news with us at 6 p.m.?'

'Fine,' I said. 'Why not? Let's do it.'

No sooner had I put the phone down when it rang again. This time it was a producer from Talksport radio station. They wanted me on in the next half an hour. We were stuck in a bit of traffic, so we did it there and then. I was in the car with Barrie and Netty, talking live on radio. When that was done, another call. It was another radio station producer wanting me on their show. He was happy to do the interview straight away, so we had a chat and that was it. Then we pulled up at the offices of Hodder and Stoughton and our next appointment. What a morning it had been!

We all went inside and met Fiona and some of the team. I didn't have the first clue how to write a book, so before I signed anything I wanted to have a chat about how it would all work. We had a wicked chat with them. I had to pinch myself that this was my life they were talking about wanting to publish. Was what I'd done so special? Would anyone want to read our story? Judging by the reaction we'd had since the story broke it appeared there was an appetite out there for it.

Barrie was getting her usual attention and, after being good as gold all morning, expressed her opinion on becoming a book cover star by promptly weeing on their carpet! Oops. Possibly the longest awkward wee ever!

After we'd talked about the book and how best to write it, the team showed us up to their roof terrace and invited us to take some time to chill out and have some lunch. The terrace had some stunning views along the river. It was a great spot for us to relax and after the exertions of the morning we needed it.

By the time Sky News sent a car for us, *This Morning* had made their own YouTube video of our appearance and it was flying all over social media. People couldn't seem to get enough of Barrie. Britain was a nation of dog lovers after all.

We arrived at Sky to find everyone knew who we were. It was like Barrie's videos were on every phone. She was really tired, which wasn't a bad thing as it meant she was very calm. She needed to be. At one point we had about twenty people standing around us wanting to pat her. I was becoming quite the veteran of live broadcasting and, just like it had been on *This Morning*, we sailed through it without any hassles. When the time came to pile into the car that would take us home, we all collapsed into the back, exhausted. We got home at 11 p.m. and were all absolutely shattered. What a day it had been. It felt like Barrie was the most famous dog in Britain right now!

21

We were all so tired we slept until about 11 a.m. the following day. The previous day had taken a lot out of all of us, so we had a lazy time, getting our heads round the craziness of the last twenty-four hours. I wanted to use the time to read a few of the messages I'd received throughout the day; there were so many and this moment of quiet was the perfect time to just sink into it all. Some of the messages really struck a chord, as they came from fellow veterans. Some had heard of my story from the papers or the media, others through word of mouth.

One soldier said they saw my *This Morning* interview and what I'd gone through resonated with them deeply. They asked me for advice on how to overcome some of the challenges they were facing. They struggled to be a civilian, just as I did, and they didn't know if they had a purpose in life beyond that of a military man.

It moved me deeply to read these messages, and I felt compelled to help out, even if just by speaking about what I'd gone through, and the little I knew. There was an innate feeling of responsibility within me to protect a fellow soldier. I felt confident, for the first time, talking about my experiences. I could only offer advice based on what I knew, and the more I vocalised my own feelings, the more I began to understand them myself. Before I knew it, I'd been replying to messages for about an hour. It felt like it was my duty to speak out; to make sure people knew they were not alone in this.

I'd felt alone for so long and, if not for Barrie, I probably would have continued on that path of loneliness until I couldn't continue any longer.

Barrie enabled me to help others, because she helped me.

Tomorrow was Remembrance Sunday and a good time to reflect. I didn't do parades. I think I'd only ever done one before. I couldn't get involved in one this time, as I'd already said I'd go over to Powerwave gym in Bromley, south London, and help them with videos and photos they were doing.

I had to be there at 10.30 a.m. and Netty and Barrie came with me. As usual, everyone was fussing over Barrie. She was getting a little better around people, so I took the opportunity to take myself off to a corner, get my phone out, and watch the Armistice Day parade on TV. The whole thing about Remembrance Sunday, with the 'Last Post' and the rest of the music, sends me into a really weird mental headspace. So I just sat in the corner and watched it on my own. Barrie and Netty were fine without me, meeting people and chatting, so I had that moment on my own to remember everything. During the two-minute silence I said a quiet prayer for those who didn't make it back, who weren't as lucky as me. When it was over I shut my phone off and got on with the work.

Helping out at Powerwave was a good distraction from the commemorations, but when we were finished we headed back to Hornchurch and took a walk to the church at the top of the hill where the town's war memorial is situated. We sat for a bit and had another moment of reflection. One or two people walked by while we sat.

'Excuse me.' We looked up to see a couple standing by us. 'Hope you don't mind us disturbing you but we just wanted to say your dog looked like one we saw on TV.'

Netty and I exchanged a look. No way! Was Barrie so famous she was being recognised off the telly?

'This is the dog that was on TV,' Netty said.

The couple laughed. It was the first time they'd ever approached a famous dog before! It was a lovely light moment to transport us back to the present. But in my moment of contemplation a seed had been planted – something I'd have a chat with Mitch about developing over the coming weeks.

I was going to throw myself back into Beyond Limits but I still had some things to get on top of with Barrie. She was still very disobedient and was proving difficult to train. She didn't like being apart from Netty and me at all. She'd jump at the door, scratching, doing anything to get through it to get to us.

It was understandable, but the events of the last week had shown us that our curious pup needed a lot more care than

I had originally thought and it was a challenge for Netty and me. One of our clients, Tracey, owned Barehams, a doggy day care not far from us, and ran obedience classes. So we took Barrie over to the day care, because if there's one thing Barrie loves it's other dogs. She is definitely a pack animal and loves running around with them. We took her over there for a couple of days and started doing classes with their trainer Andy. He was so good. He took the time to understand Barrie and listened to her story. He studied her with me and watched as, even on the lead, when I asked her to do something she looked at me as if to say, 'No, why am I on a lead and why would I want to do that?'

After our first class he pulled me aside.

'I think I understand her personality,' he said. 'She thinks she's the leader of your pack but she's still so very young she doesn't really know *how* to lead the pack. So she's just doing random stuff'.

I laughed. He'd got her bang on.

'She's basically like a teenager wanting to be in charge.'

That was exactly right. Netty and I had both felt it was like living with an adolescent.

He gave us tiny things to do every week, just simple commands that, crucially, we had to stick to and be consistent with so she'd learn to follow them.

Over the following weeks she started to show signs that she understood she didn't have to protect us all the time.

'She needs to know she comes lower in the pack than you and Netty!' Andy said.

Hmm, I thought. That might take some time.

At least, though, with Andy's help we had something to work with. We were on our way. But, he said, we still had to keep her on the lead for months until we were sure she wouldn't run off. So we had an intensive period of training Barrie all over again and studying her needs.

During this time our story was still flying around the internet. We'd agreed to let The Dodo help, as they said they could promote Barrie's profile. They made their own video about us and, boy, were they true to their word. When that went out it was bigger than when the story went live on TV. My phone didn't stop for about two weeks afterwards. My Instagram, Facebook, everything, just exploded.

Netty continued to update Barrie's own Instagram account and her followers were soaring by the day.

It was a lot of fun watching her get so popular but we had a moment of seriousness when one day she stopped eating. It was so unlike her to go off her food; she had me worried. Was it a delayed reaction to her journey? Had we done too much, too soon?

When we'd taken her to the vets, not long after her live TV day, they had checked her paperwork, looked over her vaccinations. Everything was in order. While she was with War Paws she was given the injections she legally had to have before being allowed into the UK, so anti-flea, rabies, all that sort of stuff. She had her blood taken every three months to make sure she didn't have any blood-borne diseases that she could bring to the UK. The vet said she was on target for weight but did advise that she perhaps needed a little bit of weight on her, so we'd been feeding her up a bit. To see her stop had the alarm bells going.

It turned out we were worrying for nothing – Barrie is just fussy! Maybe the diet she was on in Syria was to blame after all. Her tastes had become too cultured. It's interesting that she remembered that aspect of her time there, but not the training! Funny that. Anyway, the solution was to change her food after every couple of weeks before she got bored of it.

As life with Barrie began to settle into something resembling normality, I threw myself into work. If Barrie was my baby, Beyond Limits was my second child. As a soldier I was stupidly stubborn; if I set out to do anything, I was determined to see it through – no matter what. Even with Barrie Watch; the moment I thought to myself I was bringing her home, I was bringing her home. That was just how it was.

Beyond Limits might not have been profitable for years but recently it had been establishing its own identity. When Mitch and I founded Beyond Limits as a soldier and fireman who wanted to do something good for our community, in 2016, we didn't know how to do it. The thing is, as we grew, so did the company. We both had to acknowledge where we felt we needed to work on ourselves, and we did.

We became more vocal about the different emotions we were going through. We said fuck it to that British stiff upper lip that had kept us muted for so long. We were men, and it was okay for us to be vulnerable.

I think all this newfound attention and what it brought – a bounce and confidence that I didn't have before – allowed Mitch and me to change the way we approached training. It wasn't about lifting heavy weights; it was about lightness of mind. I spoke to many soldiers in the weeks that followed Barrie's and my appearance on *This Morning*, and I joined podcasts to speak about the issues that plagued our community.

One soldier spoke candidly; he had trained all his life but never been to a war zone. He, much like myself, was an outcast growing up. He was repeatedly told he wasn't good enough, until the words, in his mind, became true. He felt guilty, he said, that he couldn't speak about his struggles after leaving the army because, unlike a lot of us, he'd never stepped foot in a war zone. But his war zone was someplace different entirely.

These conversations made me grow in leaps and bounds as a person, because I could listen to new perspectives and, in understanding other people's struggles, I was resolving my own.

This lad never went to war, but when he left the army he felt all the things I felt. That lack of confidence, the constant doubt, the fear of rejection, the need for a routine. He was completely crippled by this anxiety that he couldn't live his life the way he wanted. He felt alone, and I couldn't help but

221

laugh, as it seemed like so many of us feel alone in a situation that we all shared but never felt comfortable revealing to each other.

I told Mitch I didn't want to just help people who suffered with PTSD, I felt compelled to help anyone I could. Beyond Limits wasn't going to be a fitness company to get people ready for the summer in Ibiza, it was going to help people who were down – just like I was, just as this soldier was, and just as Mitch was – grow in confidence, and become the person they could be. This was the germ of the idea I'd been mulling over. Unearth that potential, and push people beyond what they thought they were capable of.

'If you can't train yourself, who can you train?' I asked Mitch as we finished another day in the gym. Our client list was ever-growing, and was into the hundreds by this point. It might not sound like much, but for us it meant the world. As I said, I was stupidly stubborn. Beyond Limits should have never survived beyond 2016. It was led by two mates who knew nothing about business. But we were never going to let this company fail, even if it meant losing everything. I'd spent a week living in my car, running the company from the backseat. I wasn't going to give it up now. This was a no-fail mission.

Mitch and I developed the 3XB system. Build, Burn, and Beyond. We took both of our experiences and applied all that we learned – this is something we pushed onto people as well. Always be ready to adapt, and always be ready to learn.

It would have been unfathomable to me in the past to see the way I approached speaking to people now. I used my own struggles to show people that there was strength in all of us. I let myself appear weak, because we cannot allow the appearance of weakness to limit us from progress. I wasn't afraid to appear weak any more, because that wasn't actually weakness.

So many people who walked into our gym hated the way they looked. They needed to look different. Some felt embarrassed to come in, because they didn't want to make a fool of themselves. They lacked confidence.

I doubt many of the people who came to our gym shared my path. None of them went to war, none of them saw the things I saw. Yet, we all shared similar emotions. Similar insecurities.

Build. Burn. Beyond. This was our new mantra. Barrie enabled me to build, burn and go beyond what I thought was achievable. Those three stages were a loose outline that stemmed from the growth Barrie enabled me to go through.

One afternoon we took three mums up to Snowdon, in Wales. They'd completed the first two stages of 3XB. Build, which were basic workouts, nutrition and fundamentals. And burn, which was applying all you'd built to gruelling training sessions where they went flat out. They were now ready to go beyond.

These three mums were about to join me in a race, a marathon, up the mountain. When we reached the base, we looked up and Snowdon towered over us. You could barely see its snowy white peak, but that was our goal. I pointed up.

'Ladies, that's where we're going.'

Our path was a scramble up Crib Goch through Pen Y Pass. The toughest way up Snowdon. At its peak was the whitest of whites.

I was met with a few nervous chuckles, but we were going to do this. The weather wasn't on our side – a biting wind guzzled up the Welsh sky that afternoon, but that just added to the sense of adventure.

We began our ascent, jogging up the sides while we could. Soon, they would become steep, and we would need to begin climbing.

'Don't stop. Keep going!' I bellowed. The only response was loud panting and a few audible groans.

It was never meant to be easy. But then, it got a little harder. As we inched closer towards the summit, the mountain grew steeper and steeper. Each step forward carried more weight than the last.

Legs began to give up about 1,500 feet into our ascent.

'Keep going, ladies. You can do this,' I yelled. The weather continued to worsen, with a torrential rain quickly looming above us. Pellets of hail shot down from the sky. Our boots and socks were soaked and muddied. It reminded me of being in Afghanistan. How we always felt wet and cold. These mums were not military-trained, but they were doing a hell of a job on that day.

Nearly two hours into our vertical marathon, we were told we couldn't go any higher and that we had to go down as it was becoming too dangerous to climb. The ladies all breathed a sigh of relief – truthfully, so did I. We were destroyed by this point; our legs had given way, we were sore and we were freezing.

On our way down we approached a lake. We were at the top of a cliff with a drop below. One final task. I looked at these three mums, and they shook their heads at me.

'There's no way I'm doing that!' said Kate, trying her best to avoid looking down. As she inched towards the edge of the cliff, some tiny rocks trickled off the side and fell into the lake.

'No way, man.'

'You can do it, Kate.'

'I can't.'

'You can.'

'No. I can't.'

'On three, Kate. C'mon.'

She had a look of terror on her face as she held my hand. We looked down into the endless blue beneath us. Then, on three, we jumped.

The elation on their faces and the excited chatter afterwards told me all I needed to know. They could do it – and they had.

22

'Sit, Barrie. Sit, sit, sit . . .'

Barrie's tail wagged uncontrollably. The clouds of winter hung above our shed as sleety rain fell like icy bullets onto the frosty grass. Christmas lights, flashing bright red and green, swung across the roof like vines latching on to walls and pillars. She tried to catch the shards as they dropped to the ground, barking in excited stupefaction as the once-solid frost quickly turned to water on her face.

She was so happy; her first Christmas was approaching. Our first Christmas.

Barrie had been with me for nearly two months, the best two months of my life. Initially, we were somewhat co-dependent. Something that wasn't necessarily healthy, but it was necessary. We needed each other to survive. Barrie and I were kindred spirits; I saw in her many of the same hardships and experiences I'd gone through.

She still struggled a bit, like she was still acclimatising to her new life. Not just to her surroundings, but also to herself. We had to remember she was a street dog, born in a war zone, surrounded by rubble and wreckage. She had spent most of her life being transplanted from one place to another, sometimes in the back of a truck, other times in the darkness of an aeroplane's cargo hold. Her instincts were always to survive and protect. Now, she was free, but it was a strange sort of freedom and still one she wasn't used to. She didn't like being confined to a lead. She still didn't know what that meant. She was an animal, not a pet. She didn't want to stay indoors, she wanted to run wild. I think she struggled with her own identity. We worked on it, every day. I knew she needed to get out as much as possible, so it became part of my routine to take her on long walks, but we all felt they wouldn't be the same until she could run free. Two months on, though, it was still a risk. She had a lethal combination of being smart – and fast. If we let her off the lead the chances were she'd take off, get the scent of something and if either of us called her she'd think, 'Yeah, whatever.'

Each morning began the same way the previous morning had. We woke up next to each other, Barrie would sit on my chest, I'd wrestle her off me for a good minute. We'd go for a walk, and then we'd shower. Well, *some of us* showered. Some of us flailed around, convulsing, while Daddy was forced to bear-hug them into the bath. I won't name names, but only one of us has scratches and bruises all over their body. Barrie followed me to work, where she was always the centre of attention. She grew to become even more of a diva and was becoming a proper 'Essex girl' more quickly than anticipated. She'd moan and groan if even for a split second anyone placed attention elsewhere and, most of the time, she got what she wanted.

If she were good, we'd go on a country walk or at least go to one of the parks near the house, where she always befriended every dog that crossed her path. She continued to be so social, something everyone noted. She surprised people; they thought she'd be skittish due to her adverse background, but Barrie hasn't been afraid of anything. She hasn't had issues with big crowds, loud bangs, thunder. She's taken it all on the chin.

She has been teaching me, as much as I've been teaching her – which, to be fair, at this point was limited. Playing dead was still a work in progress.

I learned to be sociable, just as she was. I saw the way she interacted with everyone, and how she drew everyone to us. Before Barrie, I felt like I was on this long lonely road where being myself was never enough, and I shut myself away from anyone – friends, family or strangers. Barrie forced my hand; I had to become comfortable with myself, and realise that I wasn't this failure that I'd always believed myself to be. Each day in the gym, she would attract the attention of a new person and I'd have the opportunity to chat with someone I'd never have spoken to otherwise.

More than anything, I realised that there was kindness out there that I was denying myself because I didn't want to open up to the world. People reached out to me to thank me for what I'd done but, more than that, they spoke about how the story affected them; they shared their own vulnerabilities and sensibilities with me, someone they didn't know. It felt like everyone was my friend.

People loved Barrie so much, I started seeing my postman more often than I saw my friends. One of the biggest and strangest things that happened was that she became what was known as an 'Instagram dog influencer'. That meant she was really, *really* famous on Instagram. And we got a lot of free stuff because of it.

Almost every week I was signing for a package – gifts for Barrie, ranging from food, the expensive kind we couldn't afford, to collars, toys and just about anything a dog could hope for. These came from companies who contacted us asking if Barrie would model their products on Instagram, in the hope other dog owners would be inspired to buy such stuff for their pets. Other gifts came from complete strangers from all over the world who were so moved by what Barrie represented, they felt they needed to go out of their way to express it.

With Christmas just around the corner, the last thing Barrie needed was more gifts, but the Laidlaw family was getting into a joyous and festive mood. Aside from the corny lights that hung by my shed, a modest tree was propped up in the living room. Beneath it were gifts for everyone in the family, and – as Barrie had already sniffed out – there was a little section under the tree just for her. Mum didn't need much of an excuse to spoil Barrie. After her initial reservations, she now viewed her as a four-legged grandchild and was the worst for secretly passing her little treats.

So, as Barrie was now definitely one of the family, we made her a knitted Christmas jumper too, to make sure she didn't feel left out.

A week or so before Christmas, on a brisk Sunday morning, I was in the kitchen with Dad. We shared a cup of tea, as I searched the fridge to find something to eat. There were some kielbasa sausages that Netty had bought, a perfect treat for both Barrie and me. By now Barrie was spending a lot of time in the house with us, and so far she hadn't aggravated Dad's allergy as much as we'd feared. Plus, Dad didn't like leaving Barrie out there alone, even if it meant his allergy flared up.

Barrie curled up in her bed, which was by his feet.

'This is new?' he said.

'What?'

'The bed,' he said, pointing down towards his feet.

'Ah yes, sent by one of her many fans on Instagram.'

'Fans . . . on Insta-what?'

'-Gram. Instagram.'

Netty's page for Barrie – *Barrie the War Dog* – had amassed over 10,000 followers by December and had far more followers than myself – not that I was jealous. What's hers is mine, that's how it works. Her followers are also my followers.

As I've said time and time again, the internet is a funny old thing. The Instagram page had allowed us to connect with all the people who wanted to hear more about Barrie's story, and Netty was so good at conveying Barrie's sassiness and diva attitude in her captions. It was hard enough for me to understand, but try explaining it to Dad.

'It's all from Barrie's page. Netty does the funny captions where it looks like it's Barrie that's posting them,' I told him. 'She posts pics of Barrie looking silly with a caption like, "I love it when Mummy gives me treats or Daddy takes me for walks".'

'Mummy and Daddy, huh?' Dad replied, raising a brow while continuing to sip his tea.

'Yeah, something like that.'

'So, what's going on with you and Netty? She's spending *a lot* of time here.'

Mum's gossip senses must have been tingling, because she came downstairs and joined us just in time for us to talk about my love life, or lack thereof.

'We're great friends. Really great friends,' I said. 'She loves Barrie as much as I do.'

'Yeah, I'm sure she's staying over all of those nights because of Barrie,' Mum quickly interjected.

I laughed, but I'd be lying if I said I hadn't thought about it either. Netty and I had an interesting relationship – we were friends, and then we became parents to this beautiful dog. We still hadn't spoken about it, but we spent all our time together, we just never put a label on what we were to each other.

'I also spent all that time with your mum before we got together because I wanted to be around her dog,' Dad replied.

A family of comedians, I thought. Ha, ha.

Truth be told, I wasn't sure if I was ready to get into a relationship. The past few months had been some of the best months of my life, and I didn't want to mess anything up by doing anything drastic.

'She's good for you, Sean,' Mum said. 'Don't let her go.'

This Christmas felt particularly special to me. Barrie was around, Rachel's daughter little Sophie as well, and all the family. It felt like we were all in a good place for the first Christmas in a long time. It wasn't fancy, quite the opposite. We had a tree with some presents beneath it – most of which were for Barrie.

My family are big into 'secret Santa', so we only buy one present for one person. My one Christmas present from my family was from my brother-in-law, Gemma's husband Alex. I opened it – and I couldn't believe my eyes. It was a bed for Barrie! My only present for Christmas, and it's for Barrie!

Our dinner was simple; the turkey wasn't too dry, and the rice pudding wasn't too sweet. We wore silly jumpers just like anyone else would. But I had a lot to be thankful for this Christmas. I was thankful that my family was so patient with me when I was at my lowest point, and that they were here with me now, to enjoy the highs.

Raucous laughter made for the soundtrack of the evening. Barrie seemed to love Christmas. She kept running around the house, clad in her red Christmas jumper whose colour matched most of our hot flushed cheeks, and began snooping under the tree for her gifts.

Netty stopped a moment to take a picture.

'A Christmassy photo for the 'Gram,' she announced.

She uploaded it to Instagram, wishing everyone a Merry Christmas on behalf of Barrie and the rest of us, with some additional hashtags for good measure.

I left the living room and bumbled into the kitchen where it was quieter. Netty joined me. We sat next to each other; her head rested on my shoulders.

'A woman messaged us on Barrie's account,' she said, interrupting the silence. 'She wants to go on a date.'

'With Barrie?'

'With you.'

'Oh,' I replied. 'Is she hot?'

I could tell Netty didn't appreciate the joke.

'She can stay away. You're mine.'

'Am I?'

'Yes.'

For once I didn't feel the urge to argue, because she was right. She wasn't going to let it drop this time, though.

'So tell me,' she said.

'What?'

'Are we boyfriend and girlfriend?'

I couldn't help laugh. It was so comical with her cute Polish accent.

'Yes!' I said.

'Good,' she said, nodding. It was all she needed to hear – for now maybe at least.

Once the festivities were out of the way we made plans to visit her family over in Poland in January. All of Netty's family are there. I'd only met her dad once, when he came into the gym. We'd been together so long now that it felt right to make the effort to go and see them. I didn't really want to take Barrie, although we could have driven over with her. I've had a few people wanting to pay to fly Barrie and me over to loads of places, like America, but I always said no. Barrie has done so much travelling already and I just wanted her to be somewhere for a while.

Netty's home is in Elblag, near Gdańsk, and in January it was absolutely freezing. Her family is very outdoorsy, so even though it was winter we still went to the beach. I couldn't believe it. The water was like ice. It was ridiculous. Aside from that factor, however, it was amazing to meet her family and friends and get a sense of where she is from.

Netty took me out for a meal with her friends so she could show off her new English boyfriend! When I was a soldier I used to consider my drinking stamina to be very high, but with my new life I had pretty much given up alcohol. I still drank but only when we went out. The meal started normally and everyone spoke English, which was great. As the night wore on, though, the Poles started to step it up a gear. Out came four bottles of vodka, along with the beers. Netty explained the custom is to sip the vodka shot while you drink your beer. That didn't last long, particularly when one of her friends, Lukasz, and I started talking about our military experiences. He had been conscripted as Poland still had national service. We were shooting the vodka and drinking the local Tyskie beer like it was going out of fashion! My next memory was waking up at 2 p.m. the next day, much to the amusement of Netty's family. I had managed to hold my own with the drinking, as we went through five bottles of vodka and God knows how many beers but it was the next day I let myself down. I wasn't sick, which was good, but I was dead to the world. I finally rose at about 6 p.m. to be told I had to go and meet Netty's grandparents. That was tough!

In all, I met her nan, granddad, mum and dad. They don't speak English, but they all seemed really cool, from what I could gather from Google Translate! It's a beautiful part of the world and Netty and I talked about how great it would be to return with Barrie and explore the many forests and mountains around where she grew up. Hopefully, before 2019 is out we will get a chance to drive back and embark on a Polish adventure. I think Barrie would love it there.

I seem to have made an impression with Netty's mum because, after we came home, she started texting me every couple of days. In one message she said how happy she was to see how Netty was with me. Netty moved to the UK with someone she was with for fourteen years but she didn't have an easy time of it. Her mum said she never thought she'd see her so happy. That's a lovely thing to hear. We're quite the little unit, Netty, Barrie and me. We've all needed saving at some point.

Going to Netty's homeland was a very special moment for us. And we had another not long after we returned to England.

Barrie was going to be one and, although we couldn't be sure of her actual birthday, we decided to mark the

SEAN LAIDLAW

anniversary of the day I rescued her from the rubble – 28 February.

We like the BrewDog pub in Tower Hill, in London, and because the company has 'dog' in their name they allow our four-legged friends in all their bars. We were in there having a drink and discussing what we could do to mark Barrie's birthday when they said, 'You could have it in here.'

A birthday party for a dog . . . in a pub? A year earlier I would have said such a thing was insane. However, after a few months of living with a famous dog my attitude was turned 180 degrees.

That's because one of the maddest things to happen since Barrie became an 'Instagram dog influencer' was that we had owners of other famous dogs asking if we wanted to meet up and have a coffee.

My first thought was, 'No way. I bet they'll be dog weirdoes.'

We have been invited to a couple of dog events and I knew the type – the people who thought they were famous because their dogs were. The type that walk around saying, 'Oh, Mitsy can't have any gluten.'

It wasn't really me and I was a bit apprehensive. But Netty persuaded me to go along and, to my surprise, we met a group of people who were perfectly normal. So, among others, we've got to know Nick, who owns Puggy Smalls, Paz and Jake, who created 'All About Lloyd' in honour of their pooch, and Anna and Giovanni, the 'parents' of Buzz. We've got Charlie who owns Pop Sausage, we hang out with Dan and Ben, the 'dads' of LV Poms, two Pomeranian twins called Louis and Vinne and then there's Dean and Ellie who own The Cardashians. They've all become Barrie's best mates. We've got a group of six or seven dogs and partners we meet up with every other week.

So, when it came to Barrie's birthday, Netty put out a few invites and from there it escalated. On the day we had thirty or forty dogs there. We had a cake for Barrie with the front cover of this book on it, we had special cupcakes and cookies for dogs, 'beer' and 'prosecco' for dogs. All the dogs came in little outfits. One dog was in a tutu! And of course the whole event was recorded for posterity and posted on Instagram.

It was chaos and completely mad, but also life-affirming and a whole heap of fun.

At one point Barrie proceeded to wee, in front of everyone, on the floor of the BrewDog pub. There was no way of hiding it. She has no shame!

We let all the dogs eat the cake at the same time, which was when we discovered Barrie had learnt a new skill from her mum Netty – only child syndrome! She was not happy in the slightest, particularly when she saw Puggy Smalls making light work of a cake twice his size!

At one point, as I was surrounded by all these crazy-looking dogs, I scanned the room. I saw Netty having a laugh. I saw Barrie in a little denim jacket surrounded by her best mates, looking like a kid having a ball at her first birthday party.

And you know what, I thought, I wouldn't change this for the world.

Epilogue

Who would have thought finding that dusty little creature buried in the rubble would have had such a profound effect on my life – on so many lives?

I often think about that day. How if it wasn't for the type of job and the training that I had, I might not have been attuned to the cries of a helpless animal. I might have walked right by her and not have noticed. We might not have been in that area to find her. I don't know if it was luck or fate or the universe meant for us to be.

All I know is that Barrie came at the right time. At another time in my life I might not have been open to taking her in. After all, I've been to Bali, Vietnam, Afghanistan . . . I've met many stray dogs, but I've never brought one home. Why this dog, why then, why now? Those are the big questions.

What a year or so it has been. It's crazy. I was at a dog event recently (we get invited to a lot!) and I was sitting with fellow dog dads Nick and Charlie. All these dogs were running around. Barrie was just sitting there chilling. Nick turned to me and said, 'How mental is it that a year ago you were in Syria blowing shit up with Barrie by your side and now you're sat at a dog festival near London and Barrie is wearing a denim jacket.'

He was right! How do you begin to process that? I know I can't. It is just crazy what we've come from to this. I have to pinch myself sometimes to check this is really happening.

I'm not saying it's all plain sailing. I still have moments from time to time when I can feel the tension building, like when the company has a deadline and I'm worried we're not going to hit it. Or a VAT bill comes in and I get stressed out. But, this time it's different. Previously that used to lead somewhere but now it doesn't. I can come home now and forget it. Work doesn't have to follow me home any more. Before, I would come home and I wouldn't eat and I couldn't sleep and the stress would build and build. Now I have Netty to help calm me down and make sure I eat a proper dinner even if I do have to sort out some work stuff. It doesn't get on top of me now. And on the odd occasion when I can feel myself getting anxious, I close my laptop and play with Barrie outside.

So much has happened in the time I met Barrie. So much to be thankful for.

In April, more out of necessity than anything else, I applied for a job with the local ambulance service. Don't get me wrong, Beyond Limits is doing really well now and since Barrie's come home I think it's grounded me. Mitch and I are slowly getting better and learning all the time about how a business is run. It's come on tenfold and is making good money but we don't want to take any money out. So I decided to get a job but, me being me, I couldn't just have any job. I was looking for the sort of job that *I* could do, with the training I have. One day an email came in from the forces recruitment service saying the ambulance service were recruiting in my area. It turned out they are based two buildings down from my gym. I applied for it and, with my military qualifications, got the job the next day. I now work as an ambulance care assistant, which is essentially the paramedic's assistant, which is basically a very expensive Uber taxi service for people who are very ill! I do four days on, four days off, so that works out as four days with the ambulance service and four days at the gym. Given the nature of the job, I have had to deal with the odd serious incident, but where my mind is now I am a lot more comfortable in my life and I feel I can handle these challenges a lot better.

Barrie has grounded me and I am happy with Netty. Being back in uniform has helped, as has the feeling of pride in the job I do.

Barrie is still a work in progress, but we are getting there. We've got her – finally – to accept, albeit reluctantly, that she comes below me in our pack of three. We just need to teach her that Netty is also above her in the pack! That could take a while yet.

Barrie still needs to realise that when we're out on walks she stays by our side and doesn't run off. She's had a few moments when she's taken off around a corner to sniff something and we've had that heart-stopping moment: 'Oh shit, she's run off.' Usually it involves me sprinting after her. I'll turn the corner and she'll be sitting there looking at me, as if to say, 'What?'

She continues to be an Instagram star. Due to her status we are inundated with dog products. She has her own wardrobe full of clothing, including denim jackets, even military gear. It's ridiculous, frankly.

However, there are other huge benefits. In March we were invited to Crufts in Birmingham, where we received VIP passes and were interviewed by Clare Balding on live TV. All our dog friends were there and it was great to meet them all again.

As we've been doing a bit more travelling, we thought we'd treat ourselves to a new car and went big with a Mercedes GLC SUV. I built a boot space with metal grating for Barrie. For the first week she looked as though she couldn't really understand why she was in a boot instead of the backseat, but she's grown to like it. There's enough space for her to lie down and chill out or stand up and look out of the windows. An added bonus is that the windows are blacked out in the back, so she can see out but no one can see in. As she's still very protective about us, particularly when people come up close, it's been great because people don't come up to the car as much to look at her, so she's much more relaxed.

Being more content work-wise, and having Barrie settled, it's probably unsurprising that I'm much happier at home. It's unbelievable to me how much that dog has done for me, it's like a butterfly effect – or *Barrie effect* – that has brought me continued and unbridled joy.

At the start of this story I was lost and now I have found a dog that's taught me more about myself than I could possibly imagine.

And, in Netty, I've found someone I want to spend the rest of my life with.

When you realise you have met that someone you want to make it official. And so I did.

I didn't want ours to be any normal proposal. I wanted it to be special. And I wanted everything to be just right.

Now Netty being Netty meant I had a few issues to consider. Firstly, she doesn't like being the centre of attention. I knew, come the publication of this book, there might be a launch party. That might have been the perfect opportunity to pop the question, but being in front of a roomful of people might have been too much for Netty. She might have got embarrassed in front of people she knew and never forgiven me!

My other dilemma was what to do about a ring. I wanted to pick one myself so I could present it to her when the time was right. And I wanted to make sure it was the right size. Netty doesn't really like wearing jewellery. Whenever we've tentatively spoken about potential engagement or wedding rings she said she wouldn't wear one. So I was out on a limb. I knew that whatever I chose couldn't be over the top. I didn't want to risk getting her something she didn't like. With that in mind I looked at a few designs and decided something simple but sparkly was the way to go.

When Netty and her friend Paige booked a holiday to Marrakesh in spring I saw an opportunity to start laying the groundwork. I asked Paige to discreetly have her try on some rings to see what size I'd need to get. She did so. Next I had to settle on the design. I had about three designs I liked so I showed them to Paige to get her opinion. Netty, I'm sure she won't mind me saying, has short little fingers – little sausage fingers I call them! I did some research online and found out that pear-shaped diamonds are perfect for her length of finger. I settled on a design with a centre pear-shaped diamond with smaller diamonds on each side.

I was still deciding on when best to propose when Netty suggested we take a short break in June – just a five-day break between my shifts, meaning I'd only have to take one day's holiday. She found a hotel in Corralejo, on Fuerteventura, one of the Canary Islands, and went ahead and booked it.

When I go on holiday I don't like just sitting on a beach or by the pool. I like to get out and see the place I'm visiting and have some adventures. So I looked up some of the excursions on offer and found one where we could go on a tour of the sand dunes on a buggy. It looked a lot of fun. I scrolled through the photos from the tour company and saw one from the top of a huge dune overlooking the sea. It was really picturesque and I thought it could be the perfect spot. I emailed the company and told them what I wanted to do. They were really excited and came up with lots of suggestions on how best to do it. They worked with a photographer and videographer on the tour who would be able to capture the moment perfectly, so they put me in touch with them.

The next phase of the operation was to get the ring and then tradition dictates that I needed to call Netty's parents, let them know what I was planning and, hopefully, get their blessing. This wasn't going to be easy as neither her mum nor dad speak

English, so I enlisted the help of another of her friends, Beata. The week before we went away, I video-called her parents and got Beata to join in the call to translate. When she told her parents they both started crying and immediately said 'yes' and gave the thumbs up to the camera. It was so sweet.

I had to get the ring out to Fuerteventura without Netty spotting it. The dune buggy tour was booked for the Saturday. I wanted to book a restaurant for that night when we'd – hopefully – have something to celebrate. I'd been looking online before we left but I didn't want to book somewhere that appeared to be okay in the pictures but when we got there wasn't that nice. I thought I'd wait until we got to the resort and then I'd scope out a few places. On the day before the excursion we went for lunch at the beach. As we were eating some pizza I discreetly googled some restaurants to see if I could find one that looked suitably romantic. However, from where I was sitting I could see right along the beach and saw one called Mi Casa that looked ideal. It had chairs right on the beach, the décor was nice, and there was a quaint little boat outside. How could I check it out without Netty wondering what I was up to? I had an idea.

'I need to go to the toilet,' I said.

'Okay.'

'It's a number two, so I might be some time,' I laughed.

She shook her head, laughing, and continued eating her pizza.

The restaurant was a good 300 metres away and I sprinted the whole way. As soon as I got there I knew it would be perfect. I spoke to a waitress who directed me to the restaurant owner who was there too. I told them what I was planning to do. They thought it was fantastic and reserved me the table right at the front, next to the little boat. That sorted, I sprinted back. The flip-flops I was wearing were brand new and all that running meant the straps were cutting into my feet. By the time I got back to Netty they were killing me.

'Fancy a walk along the beach?' she said.

'Eh, okay,' I said, wincing at the thought of walking any further.

'Oh my God,' she said, seeing the cuts to my feet. 'How did you get those cuts?'

'The flip-flops. They're just new. I'll be fine though.'

We walked along the beach, which of course took us past Mi Casa. The waitress and the owner were standing outside doing that awkward thing of looking anywhere else but me.

I nudged Netty. 'This place looks really nice, doesn't it?'

'Yes,' she said, noticing the chairs were nice and the little boat. 'It looks really romantic. Maybe we can go there tomorrow.'

'Yeah,' I said. 'Maybe we can.'

Everything was set. Saturday came and we went to get started for the buggy tour. I was so excited I could barely contain it. I wanted to tell Netty everything, blab it all out. After all, she was the person I told everything to. Now I had the most important thing to say but I couldn't tell her – yet!

We got the guys organising the tour and they asked for our reservation. When I told him I'd done it over email, he gave me a look, said something in Spanish to his colleague and, while Netty was distracted, gave me a wink. We were on!

We set off and the buggy tour was a lot of fun – haring up and down sand dunes. Halfway round the tour they stopped us all at the top of the largest sand dune. It was just like it was in the photo I'd seen online – but infinitely more stunning. We all took a breath and let the beauty of the location sink in.

'Right, everyone in a circle,' one of the tour guys said. Everyone looked a bit bemused but we did as we were told. 'We have to do a quick test. It's a reaction test because the dune buggies don't have great brakes. So we just need a couple of volunteers,' he said, laughing.

Netty and I don't volunteer for anything so we just stood there while he looked around the group as if trying to find the right people. He was really convincing.

'You two,' he said, looking at us. 'You look really strong. You can come over here.'

He made us stand back to back.

'Take two steps forward.'

We took two steps forward. He tapped me on the shoulder and put his thumbs up. This was it. The moment had arrived.

I turned around to face Netty's back, got the ring out, and went down on my knee. Well, you've got to do these things right.

'Go!' he said.

Netty turned around and saw me on my knee holding out a box with a ring.

'Netty, will you marry me?' I said, trying to control my voice.

Her face was a picture. It was like she was waiting for her brain to catch up with what her eyes were seeing.

Then it hit her. I was asking her to be my wife. She started to tear up.

I moved the ring a little towards her as if to say, 'Well?'

She truly was speechless – a first for her!

'Yes!' she said, laughing, then came forward to hug me. I picked her up in my arms. It was like all the love I felt for her was crystallised in that moment. I put the ring on her finger. Thankfully, it fitted.

I could hear the people around us cheering and clapping. Some came up and gave us hugs and offered their congratulations. People we'd never met before that morning. In some ways it made it more special.

The photographer, who'd been taking pictures as though she was just one of the group, had jumped forward to capture the moment and had set up a GoPro video camera to film it. It was all done so naturally though.

Once we'd had our moment we had to continue with the tour, doing loads of off-road driving up a volcano. Eventually we stopped at a bar and had time to gather our thoughts. We phoned my mum and dad, who had no idea what was happening, and told them. Then we video-called her mum and dad. It was when Netty was speaking to them that she started blubbering. She couldn't control herself. They were screaming down the phone, shouting their congratulations. Netty was in floods of tears. It was a wonderful scene. We were in a bar surrounded by people and her family were shouting random Polish words over the phone!

That night at the restaurant they gave us the best table, as promised, and had decorated it with a single rose. It was perfect.

It was then we finally had a chance to talk about what had just happened. We were going to get married! It was only now sinking in.

I had been doing so much sneaking about it was a relief to be able to tell her everything that had been going on. When Netty relived the moment on the sand dune she hadn't even noticed that everyone was round in a circle. She couldn't remember anyone else being there.

After I'd told her all the things I'd done she said: 'Are there any more surprises?'

'No!' I said.

Just then the waitress arrived with a cake with 'Congratulations!' on it.

'Oh my God!' Netty said.

'I didn't know anything about this!' I said. It was a lovely touch from the restaurant.

When we got back to the hotel, there waiting for us was a bottle of prosecco, two glasses and a note saying congratulations.

The tour company sent on the video from the proposal. It was included in the general video of the day's events for all the guests. I cut down the video on my phone to our bit and added as a soundtrack a song by the American country singer Cody Johnson called 'On My Way to You'. It's become our song. I listen to a lot of country music in the car. Netty never used to like it but she's had no choice but to over the years. That song came on once and when I listened to the lyrics, I said to her: 'This is our song.'

The lyrics say, 'All the hell I've caused', all the shit I've been through, was worth it because it led me to you. It all makes sense now because I'm here. When Netty heard the lyrics she said: 'Oh, you're right. It is our song.'

In the five years I've known Netty she has always been the rock that I've relied on. For us to end up together is the icing on the cake. Even when we were just friends, she was always the person I called. In Syria she was the person I spoke to every day, morning and night, telling her about my day. Even when I was fucking up, she was always there, reminding me I was a good person and I just needed to sort my shit out. To end up with the person who has been there by my side through everything is a dream come true. She knows every part of me and still takes me for me.

She knows all about Barrie – and all I went through to get her home with us.

It was a shame I couldn't involve Barrie in the proposal because when I look back at every other good memory I've had in the year that went by Barrie was present in every single one. Like Netty, she was there for it all. Whether directly or indirectly, she was part of all the positive changes I made in my life.

I don't know if I would have ever been able to climb out of that dark pit of despair after Afghanistan without Barrie. I don't know if I would have ever been able to acknowledge the atrocities that I witnessed as a soldier without Barrie. I don't know if I would have ever been able to be a civilian without her. I don't know if I would have found it within me to open myself up to people, and realise I wasn't alone, without her. I don't know. I don't know where Beyond Limits would be without her, if I'd be able to train people without all she enabled me to learn. I don't know if I would have ever been happy without her.

A whirlwind of events brought Barrie and me together and set us on a path that I could have never imagined. My life felt like a movie and this was the part where the main characters all lived happily ever after.

Netty will be my wife and Barrie is my best friend; she always will be. And I couldn't imagine a world without her. We don't have the perfect life, far from it. We live in a shed in the back garden of my parents' home. I'm still dealing with the many thoughts that linger in the back of my mind, but I'm dealing with it. I still spend most of my days working, and while it pays the bills, I'm not going to be buying a mansion anytime soon. But I get to do all of that with Barrie.

Our happily ever after might not be as grand as in the films, but it's more than I'd ever wanted.

Meeting Barrie was the best day of my life. She didn't know it then, and I'm not sure she knows it now, but she saved me from this sinking feeling I thought I'd never survive. Everything was dark and lonely and confused before her. I felt like I was stuck in a loop, trying to pull myself up a rope that felt infinite, and that led nowhere. Now, with her in my life, I have clarity, and a purpose.

People will say I saved Barrie's life, but the truth is she saved mine.